EARLY
CHILDHOOD
BILINGUALISM

EARLY CHILDHOOD BILINGUALISM

*With Special Reference
to the
Mexican-American Child*

Eugene E. García

UNIVERSITY OF NEW MEXICO PRESS
Albuquerque

Library of Congress Cataloging in Publication Data

García, Eugene E., 1946–
  Early childhood bilingualism.

  Bibliography: p.
  Includes index.
  1. Bilingualism.   2. Language acquisition.
3. English language—Acquisition.   4. Spanish language—
Acquisition.   5. Mexican American children—Language.
I. Title.
P115.G37 1983   420′.4261   83-5735

Manufactured in the United States of America.
Library of Congress Catalog Card Number 83-5735.
International Standard Book Number 0-8263-0661-6, cloth
                                   0-8263-0662-4, paper
First edition.

Contents

Figures

Tables

1

An Introduction
to Bilingualism

The study of language continues to unfold increasingly complex wrinkles in theories of linguistics, cognition, and socialization. What was once a study of linguistic structure has become today an interlocking study of linguistic, psychological, and social domains, each important in its own right, but together converging in broader attempts to construct and reconstruct the nature of language. These converging perspectives acknowledge the multifaceted nature of social interaction. It is proposed that investigation of diverse modalities of social communication in diverse populations will result in a more comprehensive understanding of our linguistic character.

It is within this framework that the study of bilingual acquisition becomes important. The study of bilingualism and its acquisition systematically extends the work already underway in the area of monolingualism. Within the last few years, research in language acquisition has shifted from the study of one native language (Brown 1973) to the comparative study of children from diverse linguistic societies (Bowerman 1974; Braine 1976). The present text deals with the study of young children simultaneously acquiring more than one language during the early years

1

of their lives. This issue is considered important for children acquiring languages simultaneously; it is also hoped that the study of this particular population will increase our general understanding of language development.

Native Language Acquisition: A Task Analysis

Within the last few decades, interest in language acquisition has been intense and has consistently resulted in a multiplicity of methods, terms, and, of course, research publications. I will in no way attempt to do justice to this immense body of literature, but I will attempt succinctly to summarize and discuss major trends in this field inasmuch as they relate to the basic topic of interest here. For more detailed reviews of monolingual language acquisition several other publications (some technical, others not as technical) are recommended: Menyuk 1971; Cazden 1972; Brown 1973; Lenneberg and Lenneberg 1975; Braine 1976; De Villiers and De Villiers 1978; Cazden 1980.

When we consider the observation and documentation of language, it seems appropriate to conclude that "all languages are composed of speech sounds, syllables, morphemes and sentences, and meaning is largely conveyed by the properties and particular use of these units"(Menyuk 1971). Therefore, language can be seen as a regularized system wherever it occurs. Native speakers of a language can make judgments concerning this regularity by considering whether or not any utterance makes "sense." Although the emphasis has been placed on languages' structural regularity, additional evidence (Bloom 1970; Hymes 1974) clearly indicates that the structure cannot stand alone. That is, the meaning of an utterance is conveyed by both its formal structure and the specific environment in which it occurs. We must consider the physical and social characteristics of the surrounding environment as well as particular paralinguistic characteristics of the utterance itself (the intonation, stress, speed, etc. of the utterance). These characteristics become increasingly important during the study of early language acquisition when the structure of the child's utterance is limited, but communication quite complex.

Children's acquisition of their native language can be characterized as a continuum, moving from simple one-word utterances to more complex word combinations (syntax). If one ignores the functional use of crying as the beginning of communicative competence, then single-word utterances, usually very idiosyncratic ("papa" for food), mark the first distinguishable stage of formalized language development. To move beyond this early stage, the child faces developmental tasks associated with phonology, morphology, syntax, and semantics.

Phonology   This form of information available to the infant is characterized by articulatory and acoustic features of speech sounds. Therefore, any word's (or utterance's) basic physical constituent is the sound or combination of sounds which make it distinguishable from another sound or combination of sounds. An international alphabet of phonemes categorizes the various individual speech sounds which are found throughout the world. Phonologists can therefore transcribe or code the sounds of language and, in some cases, mechanically duplicate these sounds. It is the task of the child to differentiate between the sounds in his environment, much like the phonologist, and then duplicate and structure these sound systems into communicative networks. At this level it seems crucial for the child to receive phonological input; he does not come preprogrammed for any one class of sound systems.

Morphology   Morphemes can be considered the smallest meaningful unit of speech (Cazden 1972). "Free" morphemes are the first to occur in early language. These units can stand alone: "mommy," "daddy," and so on. "Blend" morphemes develop later and cannot occur alone but must be attached to other morphemes. These include verb inflections like *ed* and *ing* and noun inflections like *s* (for pluralization and possession). Extensive studies, which have traced the development of certain morphemes longitudinally in the same children, have detailed a reliable order of development for specific morphemes in English speakers (Brown 1973; De Villiers and De Villiers 1978).

The use of morpheme development as an index of development language complexity is best exemplified by work with the now famous Cambridge children: Adam, Eve, and Sarah (Brown 1973). Evident in this research, as in more detailed research of this nature, was the clear rise in Mean Length of Utterance (MLU) over time and the individual differences across subjects in this rise.

Syntax   Syntactic rules identify sequential relationships of verbal units and in doing so describe one further systematic regularized character of language. In English we are accustomed to word strings which begin with a subject (a noun or noun phrase) followed by a verb (or verb phrase) and terminated with an object (a noun or noun phrase related to the verb). Of course, this description is only an ideal mapping of pieces we call sentences. Utterances in typical human discourse frequently exclude one or more of these units and rely on the context of the utterance to convey the proper meaning. For example, the utterance "Bill" under particular circumstances may be restated as one of a number of fully formed sentences. "Come to the house, Bill;" "Bill, look at me;" "Bill, open the door;" and so on.

Of recent interest in the study of syntax has been the development of transformational strategies (Chomsky 1965). Transformational rules, by operations such as addition, deletion, permutation, and substitution among strings of words, act to change the meaning of that string (Menyuk 1971). By the use of relative clauses and conjunctions, indefinitely long sentences can be produced by any speaker consciously or unconsciously aware of transformational operations.

Semantics   The semantic component of language might be best characterized as an individual or community dictionary of a specific individual's language or of the language of several individuals. Just as I have attempted to define phonology, syntax, and semantics in these pages, each unit of speech must be defined in order to serve any meaningful function. Definitions of any linguistic unit(s) may not be formalized in the spoken language of young children, yet they are as important to the functioning of language as formal definitions are in written prose. For instance, a child's utterance of "cucu" may be defined both for him and his audience by its function, "asking for a cookie." Confusions in definition often occur owing to the differential experience with a particular unit of speech. It is clear that this same sort of definitional confusion is also operating among adults. (For example, the term *coffee regular* in most U.S. regions indicates the absence of cream; in parts of New England, this same term specifies the addition of cream.) Countless examples such as these are readily available to each of us.

Therefore, interpretation of a sentence, such as "the girl jumped rope," requires knowledge concerning the properties of each constituent part, "girl," "jump," "-ed," and "rope." Yet the string of these parts placed together in the sentence is just as important a facet of the sentence as its individual parts. That is, the syntagmatic relationship of these parts (how they are placed in sequence) reveals significant information concerning the relationship of those parts.

Language Variability

Two terms are frequently used to describe the major diversity of language—*idiolect* and *dialect*. The first term is used to recognize each person's unique linguistic experiences and how they shape that person's individual language. A group of similar idiolects that differs from other groups with respect to phonology, morphology, or syntax identifies a dialect. It is therefore the case that "similar" dialects usually make up an identifiable language group. This in turn suggests the nonexistence of a "pure" language. Theoretically, "nonstandard" dialects can be assumed to be equally well developed and systematic. Independent from its theoretical validity, the notion of dialect equivalence with regard to development and regularization receives empirical support from the extensive research on black dialect patterns (Labov 1970). Labov and his colleagues have pointed out several systematic differences between Black English and what is normally identified as the dialect of Standard English. The research describes the verb form *be* "to indicate generally repeated action, or existential state in sentences such as 'He be with us;' 'they be fooling around.'" (Labov and Cohen 1967) An additional study by Henrie (1969) found that urban black children used unconjugated *be* ("He always be there") to express habitual meaning in a task requiring them to retell a story they heard in Standard English.

Physical, geographical separation is one variable that accounts for such linguistic diversity. Although this is a common and clearly observable explanation, dialects occur under other circumstances. For instance, the speech of mothers (or any adult) to young children differs significantly from adult speech. Snow (1972) has documented this form of linguistic differentiation as more simple and more redundant. In fact, the overall speech of young children might be considered a dialect as it is presently defined here. (It is important to note that the term *dialect* is usually constrained to the description of adult, fully mature, speech competencies.) Of major significance is that speakers develop diverse linguistic repertoires and that this is the norm, not the exception.

Owing to its importance in the investigation of social class differences in speech usage, another concept related to linguistic diversity needs to be raised here: speech code. Historically, the concept of speech code can be traced to early work of Basal Bernstein, an English sociologist who was concerned with the different linguistic styles of middle-class and working-class children in England (Bernstein 1961). The speech of these children was reportedly classified into "restricted codes" and "elaborated codes." Restricted code is characterized by indexical speech, speech that presumes some high degree of shared knowledge. Therefore, this speech is usually much shorter (in terms of utterance length) and less specific in character. The elaborated code, on the other hand, is more formal in the sense that no shared knowledge is presumed. This speech makes use of more adjectives, adverbs, and clauses. Lower-class children were described as using only a restricted code while middle-class children could switch codes depending on the environmental demands. Although these formulations are clearly still a major focus of controversy, they are discussed here to serve as an introduction to the form of linguistic diversity we shall later refer to as "codes."

For bilinguals, codes are of great importance. That is, since these individuals have two topographically distinct forms of language, how, when, and why does language switching (typically referred to as code switching) occur? Is this yet another linguistic attribute which the bilingual must be concerned with in terms of acquisition? Although an entire chapter will attempt to deal with this topic (Chapter 5), it is discussed briefly here in reference to monolingualism to stress the linguistic reality that all speakers (monolingual or bilingual) most probably are immersed in social environments that control the form of their linguistic behavior. Hymes (1974) has explicitly detailed some of the variables which must be considered in determining the code or style of the speaker and the ability of the listener to "make sense" of variations.

The first of these variables, *Setting*, refers to where and when the speech act is taking place. Children are generally allowed to be louder outside than in, for instance, and may already have learned they are supposed to whisper (or not talk at all) in church.

Participants—their age, sex, kinship, social class, education, or occupation—may make a difference. An English speaker would seldom have difficulty identifying the listener in a conversation as a young child by the speaker's grammar, word choice, and intonation (although the same style is sometimes used with pets). Many languages have different pronominal form to indicate social distance, and the sex of a speaker, to some extent, determines appropriate word choice.

The *Ends* are significant. Style sometimes depends on purpose, whether the speech act is a request, demand, query, warning, or mere statement of information.

Act Sequence refers to the prescribed form a speech act takes when it is closely controlled by the culture, as is usually the case with prayers, public speeches or lectures, and jokes. It also refers to what may be talked about in each, what can be appropriately prayed about versus what can be appropriately joked about.

The same words may express various tones, moods, or manner (serious, playful, belligerent, sarcastic). The signal may be non-verbal, such as wink or gesture, or conveyed by intonation, word choice, or some other linguistic convention.

Different verbal codes may be selected. Even a monolingual will have a choice of registers (varieties along a formal-informal continuum). Many speakers are able to choose among regional and social dialects as well. The choice is usually an unconscious one and may indicate respect, insolence, humor, distance, or intimacy.

Norms of interaction and interpretation in a speech act include taking turns in speaking (if appropriate in the speaker's culture), knowing the proper voice level to express anger, and sharing understandings about such things as what to take seriously and what to discount. It includes knowing polite greeting forms and other "linguistic manners," like what not to talk about at the dinner table.

Genres vary. Some speech acts may be categorized in formal structures: poem, myth, tale, proverb, riddle, curse, prayer, oration, lecture, editorial. Even children are often expected to know a few of the forms appropriate to their culture, including the "Once upon a time . . ." of middle-class English.

Native Language Acquisition: Theoretical Perspectives

It is this multifaceted nature of language that the developing child confronts when achieving communication competence. How does he or she tackle that task? Chomsky (1965) considers language as dichotomous in nature consisting of linguistic competence and linguistic performance. The first attribute is concerned with the speaker's linguistic knowledge, the second with the speaker's actual behavioral productions. Chomsky (1965) relegates the duties of the child to that of linguist: the child must determine from relevant data in his environment the underlying systems of rules in order to generate appropriate linguistic performances. As indicated earlier in this chapter, it does not seem appropriate to restrict our interest in language to a pure structural analysis. Yet, Chomsky's conceptualization has served as a theoretical base for much of the research now available on young children. The structure of their language and their ability to perform transformations has been of prime importance. It is true that any analysis of language acquisition must account for the almost miraculous performance of young children with respect to generative speech. That is, we must be concerned with the clear performance of children in understanding and producing utterances which they themselves have never heard. Yet, recent evidence warns us to consider the social and physical context of language (Hymes 1974) as well as cognitive-developmental considerations (De Villiers and De Villiers 1978) as these relate to the function of speech.

With these precautions in mind it is appropriate to conclude that by a very early age, children have mastered a large segment of their environment. That is, seemingly with little systematic effort on the part of parents, a child has developed a significant portion of linguistic and social interaction competency within the first four to five years of his life. The child is able to understand and produce complex forms of language at this time. Complexity is defined here in terms of the linguistic features discussed earlier: phonology, morphology, syntax, and semantics. In addition, the child is capable of code switches, or shifts, which serve further to clarify his speech productions and his understanding of his social interactions. This is the case for the native speaker of one language.

Second Language Acquisition

The study of second language acquisition must be considered here because of its applicability both theoretically and methodologically to the issue of bilingualism. This form of research has been concerned with those variables operating in the acquisition of a second language after the native language has been acquired. Investigations of young children undergoing the process of second language acquisition have been completed only recently. Research in this area has borrowed extensively from the work in first language acquisition. That is, the same linguistic features have been of interest within the same methodological framework. Specifically, procedure for accumulating data on second language acquisition has taken on two forms: samples of spontaneous speech of the individual are gathered in his second language; and cross-sectional investigations of individuals exposed for varying amounts of time to the second language are undertaken. Typically investigations of this nature make use of specific language measurement instruments designed to maximize the probability of the occurrence of certain linguistic features.

Additionally, second language acquisition research has made much use of contrastive analysis. This technique calls for the comparative analysis of Language 1 (L_1) with Language 2 (L_2) so as to identify phonological, morphological, syntactic, and semantic differences and similarities (Stockwell and Bowen 1965). This form of analysis is used to predict the relative probability of linguistic errors owing to the differences between L_1 and L_2. Therefore, if a speaker of Spanish is learning English, errors in adjective-noun syntactic placement may be frequent due to the differences in rules governing this syntagmatic relationship. Furthermore, it attempts to predict areas of positive transfer. For instance, plurals in Spanish and English are formed similarly by addition of an *s* or *es* inflection to singular nouns. (This is an oversimplification, since there are other allomorphs in each language.) In this case we might expect the L_2 learner to be able to transfer positively his past experiences with this morphological form owing to previous experience with this inflexional derivative in L_1.

Dulay and Burt (1972, 1973, 1974, 1974a, 1974b) have utilized the above methodology to investigate the types of errors made by children who are second language learners. This extensive research effort has made use of cross-sectional administration of a speech elicitation instrument, the Bilingual Syntax Measure (BSM), to study the development of specific morphological classes. The BSM attempts to elicit production of target morphemes by combining the presentation of several cartoon pictures and strategic tester dialogue. Subjects' scores are determined by considering the number of utterances in which fully formed, partially correct morphemes are either present or absent in obligatory context. Morpheme order is determined by listing scores from highest percentage of occurrence to lowest percentage of occurrence. For experimental purposes, rank orders such as these are then used to compare morpheme development from one group of subjects (say Spanish-speakers learning English) to a second group of subjects (say Chinese-speakers learning English).

These studies with the BSM have led these researchers to make the following conclusions: (1) There is an invarient order of acquisition among second language learners with respect to grammatical morphemes (as measured by the BSM). (2) Fewer than 5 percent of all English errors are directly traceable to "interference" errors—errors related to L_1 forms. (3) Children learn a second language via a creative construction process; "they gradually reconstruct rules for the speech they hear guided by universal innate mechanism. . . ." (Dulay and Burt 1974:71).

The theoretical and applied implications seem clear from these conclusions. Theoretically, it would seem that L_2 acquisition is very much like L_1 acquisition. In fact, Dulay and Burt (1974a), in a detailed analysis of the few errors which were observed during BSM administration, assigned responsibility for those errors to the "creative construction process" rather than previous

L_1, rule-governing experiences. That is, observed errors were more related to language learning rather than the influence of L_1-L_2 structure difference.

Several methodological and empirical considerations leave in doubt the conclusions drawn by the above researchers. First, the studies reported have used two techniques of considerable questionability with respect to measurement. The BSM is designed to elicit particular morpheme constructions under semicontrolled testing situations. The influence of "demand" characteristics posed by the tester, the stimuli, and the multitude of administration variables have been documented experimentally (Mercer 1973). LoCoco (1976), in a comparative study of typical methods of data collection of L_2 data, presents evidence indicating the differential infuences of these methods on the number of specific L_2 errors. In addition, Hakuta (1974) has reported a different morpheme acquisition order than that reported by Dulay and Burt. His investigations considered the acquisition of English in a Japanese five year old, but did so by collecting spontaneous speech samples on a longitudinal base.

Even more recent are data by Rosansky (1976) detailing particular L_1 effects on L_2 acquisition for Spanish-speaking children and adults acquiring English. These data strongly suggest that morpheme acquisition order in L_2 is related to L_1 morpheme similarities. Additionally, Garcia (1977), in a study aimed at an experimental analysis of L_2 acquisition in three- or four-year-old children, reported clear transfer effect owing to L_1 language training manipulations. Moreover, in a detailed comparative study of L_2 acquisition using several language assessment techniques, including the BSM, Larson-Freeman (1976) found differences in morpheme orders of acquisition with other measures excluding the BSM. Given these series of empirical results, it is impossible to conclude validly that an invariant ordering of morphemes presently occurs during L_2 acquisition (see Bailey, Madden, and Krashen 1974; Larson-Freeman 1976; Rosansky 1976 for a more detailed review of L_2 acquisition).

It is probably best to conclude that several theoretical formulations are presently available to account for the process and form of L_2 acquisition. McLaughlin (1977) best summarized the incongruencies between the theoretical and empirical by admitting the unavailability of firm conclusions pertaining to second language acquisitions. He explicitly does so by detailing the following five unsubstantiated beliefs widely held with respect to second language acquisition in young children:

1. The young child acquires a language much more quickly and easily than an adult because the child is biologically programmed to acquire languages, whereas the adult is not.
2. The younger the child, the more skilled in acquiring a second language.
3. Second language acquisition is a qualitatively different process than first language acquisition.
4. Interference between first and second languages is an inevitable and ubiquitous part of second language acquisition.
5. There is a single method of second language acquisition instruction that is most effective with all children. (McLaughlin 1978, pp. 197–205).

Such beliefs have been generated through extensions of previous work with children acquiring their native language and adults acquiring a second language. Only recently has a major research effort begun to emerge with children acquiring a second language during the ages of two to five. Therefore, it is not justifiable at present to provide an unclouded single view concerning this important developmental phenomenon. Instead, various views, each worthy of consideration, emerge. A similar representation evolves in the consideration of early childhood bilingualism.

Bilingualism
As one searches for a comprehensive definition of bilingualism, a continuum of definitional attempts unfolds. On one end of this continuum are general definitions such as "the practice of alternately using two languages" (Weinreich 1953), or "knowledge of two languages" (Haugen 1972). At the other end of this continuum are the operational definitions common to the field of experimental psychology ("subjects answered positively to questions concerning their use of two languages"; "subjects scored 90% correct on a standardized test of language proficiency in each language"; etc.). Regardless of the definition adopted for any empirical or theoretical treatment of bilingualism, it is

understood that "bilinguals" come in a variety of linguistic shapes and forms. Therefore, any definition worthy of consideration must address this built-in linguistic diversity. But to consider only linguistic diversity would be an error. Thorough definitions of bilingualism must also consider cognitive and social parameters: language or languages must not only be acquired but must achieve maturity and use within definite social contexts.

The following discussion will attempt to introduce a definition relevant to bilingual acquisition during early childhood. In doing so, early childhood bilingualism will necessarily be defined with considerations of linguistic, social, psychological, and, to some extent, physiological issues in mind. There is little doubt that bilingualism cannot presently be defined to the satisfaction of the theorist, researcher, or educator, but an attempt is necessary here on purely communicative grounds. Knowing that I might fail to meet all demands placed on this definition, I will offer the entire subject matter of this manuscript as a definition of sorts.

Early childhood bilingualism defined   The term *bilingualism* here suggests the simultaneous acquisition of more than two languages during the first five years of life. This definition requires the following conditions.

Linguistic   Children are able to comprehend and/or produce some aspects of each language beyond the ability to discriminate that either one language or another is being spoken. The intent of this condition is to confer the term *bilingualism* on children who can handle other than the most basic attributes of symbolic communication (that one set of symbols [languages] is the same or different than another). This is not a limiting condition since it allows many combinations of linguistic competence to fall within the boundaries of bilingualism (the most "simple" to be included might be the child who has memorized one or more lexical or syntactic utterances in a second language).

Social   Children are exposed "naturally" to the two systems of languages as they are used in the form of social interaction during early childhood. This condition requires a substantial bilingual environment in the location of the child's first three to five years of life. In many cases this exposure comes from within a traditional nuclear family network, but this need not be the case (relatives, visitors, and extended visits to foreign countries are examples of alternative environments).

Developmental   The simultaneous character of development must be apparent in both languages. This is contrasted with the case in which a native speaker of one language who, after mastery of that language, begins on a course of second language acquisition. (The boundaries of this definitional condition are somewhat strained due to the ongoing developmental nature of language. Therefore, it is probably the case that any child meeting the two above conditions will also meet the present one.) The present condition considers as important the presence of both psychological (cognitive) and physiological development during early childhood as they relate to bilingual acquisition.

Therefore these combined conditions define the present population of interest. It is clear from these conditions that an attempt is made to consider the child's linguistic abilities and social environment in conjunction with a developmental perspective. An idealized definition follows from the three conditions stated above: A child prior to the age of five is able to function in two languages at some level of social interaction. Prior to leaving this definition in search of meaningful data, let us consider briefly each of the conditions identified as important and therefore included as "conditions" for determining early childhood bilingualism.

Linguistically, it is necessary to borrow from theoretical and empirical work addressing native language acquisition. In doing so, the primary features of language are placed in a three-dimensional perspective. That is, each language can be characterized by phonology, lexicon, morphology, syntax, and semantics. In addition, each of these categories can be considered at receptive (ability to understand) and expressive (ability to speak) levels. Therefore, acquisition of more than one language by children must consider the mastery of each of these linguistic features across languages. As the second condition of the definition implies, the acquisition task is embedded in a social milieu. It therefore remains imperative to consider the external social variables that influence both acquisition and use of a bilingual repertoire.

The linguistic and social variables considered above can be related to any bilingual, young or old. However, our concern here is with early childhood bilingualism. Two important differences are related to the meaningful distinction between this form of bilingualism and others. First, early childhood is characterized traditionally as a time of considerable physiological development. Of special importance is the development and differentiation of neurostructures which are related to language acquisition. Second, early childhood is marked by important developments related to cognitive functioning. The interaction of cognition and language has been considered important during this period.

Physiological considerations   Lenneberg (1967) suggests that any child can learn a foreign language under favorable conditions prior to the age of five. He further speculates that the ability to do so diminishes as a function of brain differentiation at later ages. Penfield and Roberts (1959) further assert that only young children can "generate" a new center, physiologically, for a second language system. Both Lenneberg's and Penfield and Roberts's assertions are based on studies of brain lesions to the left hemisphere of the brain. At birth the cerebral hemispheres are considered to be equipotential with respect to language localization. Progressive cerebral lateralization occurs after about thirty-six months of age, leading finally to the restriction of language function to the dominant cerebral hemisphere (usually considered to be the left hemisphere) at about fourteen years of age. As the cerebral cortex matures postnatally, certain linguistic functions become increasingly restricted to the left hemisphere. Lesions of this hemisphere result in linguistic impairment whose severity is correlated with the maturity of the developing cerebral cortex.

As Jacobson (1975) suggests, "Formal linguistic analysis, divorced from its biological substrates, is unlikely to be a profitable approach to the problem of how the brain generates language and purely psychological approaches to that problem are equally unlikely to succeed." This is certainly a strong case for a keen awareness of physiological variables as they relate to early language acquisition in general and to the task of bilingual acquisition in particular. Unfortunately, the dependency of this work on brain dysfunction and the unavailability of an experimental technology for investigating causal relationships between cerebral development and language acquisition leave us with little more than an awareness of possible interrelationships.

> The task of finding causal relationships between neurobiology and language has met with serious difficulties. Cerebral localizations of language function, although a necessary preliminary step, fall short of a neurophysiological explication of language. If our expectations include such an explication, we have to admit that little progress has been made toward its realization. Indeed, it is not yet possible to describe any complex type of behavior in terms of a program of neural events, and, many decades will pass before the neurophysiological mechanisms of cognitive process in men are understood (Jacobson 1975, pp. 105–6).

Therefore, although it is incumbent on us to be aware of and empirically concerned with the physiology of early childhood bilingualism, we are left to focus only on the linguistic, social, and psychological aspects of the phenomenon. This may not be the case in the near future.

Psychological considerations   The psychological aspects of bilingualism are left untreated in the above discussion. This aspect of bilingualism in early childhood further differentiates its character from other forms of bilingualism that are not considered in our earlier definition. A specific example is the case of second language acquisition. Typically, this effort is begun after near complete development of the native language. But, early childhood bilingualism takes place during the same temporal period of native or single language development in monolinguals. This temporal period is marked by parallel development in cognitive domains. Therefore, the relationship between bilingual development and cognitive development must be considered.

Recent information in the cognitive growth area has suggested an interactive relationship between cognitive structures and language acquisition (Brown 1973). A similar interactive relationship must be considered for bilingual development during early childhood. Although direct research in this area is only beginning to emerge, its theoretical relevance has been historically noted (Leopold 1953). Ervin-Tripp (1968) summarizes some of the major differences, considered psychological, between children and adults as they relate to language acquisition:

1. Children show a great readiness to learn the language of their contemporaries in a new linguistic environment.

2. Children enjoy rote memorization, while adults prefer solving intellectual problems.

3. Adults emphasize the content of language, often neglecting its formal system.

4. Children are more perceptive to the sounds of a language, adults to its meaning.

5. Children relate more to the immediate context.

6. Children usually learn new words through sensory activity, adults in a purely verbal context.

7. Children can make linguistic abstractions—learn about structures never directly presented to them, but adults have a greater capacity to remember stated grammatical rules.

8. Children seem less subject to interference from their native systems than do adults.

In conjunction with cognitive development parameters, investigators have become increasingly interested in the relationship between bilingualism and cognitive style (learning style). Cognitive style refers to the multiplicity of approaches in which individuals process environmental (sensory) information. In this manner, cognitive style is seen as an important determinant of an individual's acquisition of the full range of behavior, including language. This concept, although initially articulated by Witkin et al. (1962), has pointed to specific cognitive factors of potential importance during language acquisition. In particular, Ramírez and Castañeda (1974) have listed specific cognitive characteristics in children which they perceive generated from the socialization practices of parents with bilingual backgrounds. These characteristics concern themselves with the differences of field independence and field sensitivity (see Ramírez and Castañeda for a detailed definition of these concepts) and have implication for bilingual acquisition in early childhood.

Research with bilinguals which has considered the potential relationship between cognitive style and the social network of the child has focused on the qualitative aspects of mother-child interaction. Steward and Steward (1973) as well as Laosa (1977) have found consistent differences between Anglo (monolingual) and Mexican-American (bilingual) mother-child interaction with respect to input (instructional interactions), placing (rate of instructional interactions), and content (form of instructional interactions). Although far from conclusive, such evidence does suggest that the interactional qualities of bilinguals and monolinguals may differ substantially. Such differences may or may not be related to the bilingual character of acquisition. But such a possibility exists.

One last psychological consideration has received critical research attention: attitudes toward bilingual acquisition. Gardner and Lambert (1972) have provided the most extensive study of attitude and second language acquisition. By asking individuals to react to audio tapes of bilingual English- and French-speakers with respect to positive and negative personality attributes, they were able to conclude that listeners made such judgments according to the language spoken and not the content of the speech sample. From these and other results, these authors speculate that authoritarian and ethnocentric attitudes by the community at large, parents, and teachers may decrease the success of second language learning. Such notions of attitude point out the potential importance of social and psychological variables during early childhood bilingual acquisition.

Conclusion

In summary, then, a definition of bilingualism specific to early childhood has been presented. It is a definition including more than pure linguistic features. Instead it is concerned with traditional linguistic features in concert with social, psychological, and to some extent, physiological parameters. Additionally, although these parameters have been discussed separately (and will be divided along these same lines in the discussions which follow), they must not be seen as static entities. Indeed, it is important to view them within an interactive perspective. That is, their individual and interactive treatment theoretically, empirically, or educationally cannot be separated. This nonstatic model introduced here and discussed in detail later (Chapter 8) will be of benefit in a clearer understanding of early childhood bilingualism.

References

Bailey, N., Madden, L., and Krashen, S. 1974. Is there a "natural sequence" in adult second language learning? *Language Learning* 24: 233–43.

Bernstein, B. 1961. Social class and linguistic development: A theory of social learning. In *Education, economy and society,* eds. A. H. Halsey, Flored, and C. A. Andersen, pp. 288–314. Glencoe, Ill.: Free Press.

Bloom, L. 1970. *Language development: Form and function on emerging grammars.* Boston: MIT Press.

Bowerman, M. 1975. Crosslinguistic similarities at two stages of syntactic development. In *Foundations of language development,* eds. E. Lenneberg and E. Lenneberg, vol. I, pp. 267–82. London: UNESCO Press.

Braine, M. D. S. 1976. *Children's first word combinations.* Monographs of the Society for Research in Child Development.

Brown, R. 1973. *A first language: The early stages.* Cambridge, Mass.: Harvard University Press.

Cazden, C. B. 1972. *Child language and education.* New York: Holt, Rinehart and Winston.

Cazden, C. 1980. *Language in early childhood education.* Washington, D.C.: NAEYC Press.

Chomsky, N. 1965. *Aspects of the theory of syntax.* Cambridge, Mass.: MIT Press.

DeVilliers, J. and DeVilliers, P. 1973. A cross-sectional study of the acquisition of grammatical morphemes. *Journal of Psycholinguistic Research* 2: 269–78.

———. 1978. *Language acquisition.* Cambridge, Mass.: Harvard University Press.

Dulay, H. C., and Burt, M. K. 1972. Goofing: An indication of children's second language learning strategies. *Language Learning* 22: 235–52.

———. 1973. Should we teach children syntax? *Language Learning* 23: 245–58.

———. 1974a. Errors and strategies in child second language acquisition. *TESOL Quarterly* 8, 2: 129–38.

———. 1974b. *Natural sequence in child second language acquisition.* Working Papers on Bilingualism, vol. 3, pp. 44–66. Toronto: Ontario Institute for Studies in Education.

———. 1974c. Natural sequence in child second language acquisition. *Language Learning* 24: 37–53.

Ervin-Tripp, S. 1968. *Becoming a bilingual* (ERIC ED 018 786).

Garcia, E. Strategies for bilingual research. In *Chicano Psychology*, ed. J. V. Martinez, pp. 141–54. New York: Academic Press.

Gardner, R. C., and Lambert, W. E. 1972. *Attitudes and motivation in second language learning*. Rowley, Mass.: Newbury House.

Hakuta, K. 1974. *A preliminary report on the development of grammatical morphemes in a Japanese girl learning English as a second language*. Working Papers on Bilingualism, vol. 3, pp. 18–43. Toronto: Ontario Institute for Studies in Education.

Haugen, E. 1972. *The ecology of language*. Stanford, Calif.: Stanford University Press.

Henrie, S. N. 1969. A study of verb phrases used by five year old nonstandard Negro English-speaking children. Ph.D. dissertation, University of California, Berkeley.

Hymes, D. 1974. *Foundations in sociolinguistics: An ethnographic approach*. Philadelphia: University of Pennsylvania Press.

Jacobson, M. 1975. Brain development in relation to language. In *Foundations of language development*, eds. E. Lenneberg and E. Lenneberg, pp. 117–39. London: UNESCO Press.

Labov, W. 1970. *The study of nonstandard English*. Urbana, Ill.: National Council of Teachers of English.

Labov, W., and Cohen, P. 1967. *Systematic relations of standard and nonstandard rules in grammars of Negro speakers*. Project Literacy Reports, No. 8, pp. 66–84. Ithaca, New York: Cornell University Press.

Laosa, L. M. 1977. Cognitive styles and learning strategies research: some of the areas in which psychology can contribute to personalized instruction in multicultural education. *Journal of Teacher Education* 38: 26–30.

Larson-Freeman, D. 1976. An explanation for morpheme acquisition order of second language learners. *Language Learning* 26: 125–34.

Lenneberg, E. H. 1967. *Biological foundations of language*. New York: Wiley & Sons.

Lenneberg, E. H., and Lenneberg, E. 1975. *Foundations of language development*. London: UNESCO Press.

Leopold, W. F. 1953. Patterning in children's language learning. *Language Learning* 18: 1–14.

LoCoco, V. 1976. *A comparison of three methods for collection of L₂ data: Free composition, translation and picture description*. Working Papers on Bilingualism, vol. 8, pp. 59–86. Toronto: Ontario Institute for Studies in Education.

McLaughlin, B. 1977. Second-language acquisition in childhood. *Psychological Bulletin* 84: 438–39.

McLaughlin, B. 1978. *Second language acquisition in childhood.* Hillsdale, N.J.: Lawrence, Friabaum Associates.

Menyuk, P. 1971. *The acquisition and development of language.* Englewood Cliffs, N.J.: Prentice-Hall, Inc.

Mercer, Jane R. 1973. *Labeling the mentally retarded.* Berkeley and Los Angeles: University of California Press.

Penfield, W. and Roberts, C. 1959. *Speech and brain mechanisms.* Princeton, N.J.: Princeton University Press.

Ramírez III, M., and Castañeda, A. 1974. *Cultural democracy, bicognitive development and education.* New York: Academic Press.

Rosanky, E. J. 1976. Methods and morphemes in second language acquisition research. *Language Learning* 26: 409–25.

Snow, C. E. 1972. Mother's speech to children learning language. *Child Development* 43: 549–65.

Steward, M., and Steward, D. 1973. The observation of Anglo-, Mexican-, and Chinese-American mothers teaching their young sons. *Child Development* 44: 329–37.

Stockwell, R. P., Bowen, J. D., and Martin, J. W. 1965. *The grammatical structures of English and Spanish.* Chicago: University of Chicago Press.

Weinreich, U. 1953. *Languages in contact.* New York: Linguistic Circle of New York.

Witkin, H. A., Dyk, R. B., Fatherson, H. F., Goodenough, D. R., and Karp, S. A. 1962. *Psychological differentiation.* New York: John Wiley & Sons.

2

Becoming Bilingual During Early Childhood

→ for early

Bilingual Acquisition: A Short Review

Certainly, one of the most impressive characteristics of child development has to do with language acquisition. It seems remarkable that within the first few years of life, drastic changes in linguistic competence can clearly be identified (Menyuk 1971). Although the exact variables influencing this development are still not evident, research in this field has been voluminous and theoretically varied (Lenneberg and Lenneberg 1975; DeVilliers and DeVilliers 1978). The main focus of this research has centered around single-language acquisition (Brown 1973) although more recent research has employed cross-linguistic analysis with children who are learning different languages (Bowerman 1975; Braine 1976). Compared to these bodies of literature, very little systematic investigation is available regarding children who are acquiring more than one language, simultaneously, during the early part of their lives.

It is common for an adult bilingual to be considered "educated" (MacNamara 1967). But, as Haugen (1972) indicated, the converse may also be true. Regardless of the social connotation of bilingualism, it is clear that a child can and does learn more than one linguistic communicative form in many societies

22

throughout the world. Although not apparent from a cursory scanning of linguistic literature, research with bilinguals is not an area of recent linguistic or psychological investigation. Ronjat (1913) reports the development of French and German in his own son. Finding few deleterious effects of bilingual development, he attributed positive outcomes to the separation of the languages. In this particular case, one parent consistently spoke French and the other German. Pavlovitch (1920) also reports the development of two languages, French and Serbian, in his son. Similarly, languages spoken by parents were distinctly separated. The languages reportedly developed simultaneously with minimal confusion. Geissler (1938) reports that as a teacher of foreign languages he had observed young children acquire up to four languages simultaneously without difficulty. Only Smith (1935), in a study of missionary families who spoke English and Chinese, reports difficulty during simultaneous acquisition. This difficulty was most apparent in the language-mixing character of the children's speech.

One of the first extensive investigations of bilingual acquisition in young children was reported by Leopold (1939, 1947, 1949a, 1949b). This author set out to study the simultaneous acquisition of English and German in his daughter. In summary, these descriptive reports indicated that although the child was exposed to both languages during infancy, she seemed to weld them into one system during initial language production periods. For instance, early syntactic productions were characterized by free mixing, although "primitive" and "incomplete." Language production during later periods (age 2.2–2.6) indicated that the use of English and German grammatical forms developed independently. Even later, as English began to predominate, German syntactic utterances seemed to be related to already acquired English structures. Leopold concluded that this influence was noticed only after acquisition of complex syntactic forms was complete.

With respect to Spanish-English bilingualism only recent research is available. Carrow (1971, 1972) has restricted her study to the receptive domain of young, bilingual Mexican-American children in the Southwest. Children (ages three years, ten months to six years, nine months) from bilingual, Spanish-English home environments were administered the Auditory Test for Language

Comprehension. This test assesses language comprehension without requiring language expression. It consists of a series of pictures representing referential categories that can be signaled by words, morphological constructions, grammatical categories, and syntactic structures. These include verbs, adjectives, adverbs, nouns, pronouns, morphological endings, prepositions, interrogatives, and syntax complexity in both languages. A comparison of English and Spanish comprehension on this task for bilinguals revealed (Carrow 1971) that linguistically, children were very heterogenous—some scored better in one language than another, others were equal in both; that a greater proportion of children scored higher in English than in Spanish; and that both languages tended to improve across the linguistic parameters measured as the children became older (this was the case even though Spanish was not used as a medium of instruction for older children in educational programs).

In a cross-sectional comparison of English comprehension among monolingual English and bilingual Spanish-English children (ages three years, ten months to six years, nine months), Carrow (1972) reports a positive developmental trend for both Spanish and English in bilingual children. Additionally, bilingual children tended to score lower than monolingual children on English measures during ages three years, ten months to five years, nine months, but for the final age comparison group (six years, nine months) bilinguals and monolinguals did not differ significantly on these same English measures. These combined results seem to indicate that at the receptive level, Spanish-English bilingual children were progressing (increasing their competence) in both Spanish and English; bilingual children tend to be heterogeneous as a group, favoring one language (typically English) over another; and bilingual children "lagged" behind monolingual children in their acquisition of English but eventually "caught up."

More recently, Padilla and Liebman (1975) report the longitudinal analysis of Spanish-English acquisition in two three-year-old bilingual children. These researchers followed the model of Brown (1973) in recording linguistic interactions of these children over a five-month period. By an analysis of several dependent linguistic variables (phonological, grammatical, syntactic, and semantic characteristics) over this time period, they observed gains in both languages. They also report the differentiation of linguistic systems at phonological, lexical, and syntactic levels. They conclude:

> The appropriate use of both languages even in mixed utterances was evident; that is, correct word order was preserved. For example, there was no occurrence of "raining está" or "a es baby." There was also an absence of the redundance of words in mixed utterances as well as the absence of unnecessary words which might tend to confuse meaning (Padilla and Leibman 1975, p. 51).

The authors also report the favoring of one language (English) over another as it relates to specific morphological forms. But, by comparing these subjects' utterances to those reported by Brown (1973) for monolingual English children and those reported by González (1970) for monolingual Spanish children, they also concluded:

> There is no evidence in the language samples that might suggest an overall reduced or slower rate of language growth for the bilingual children of this study (as compared tJ monolingual children of other studies) (Padilla and Leibman 1975, p. 51).

Interlanguage Transfer

Conclusions like the one above must be considered tentative owing to the small populations of subjects and number of utterances undergoing investigation. In addition, these studies have not addressed the more specific interactive nature of bilingual development, that is, the influence one language might have on the other. When referring to this transfer phenomenon between the languages of the bilingual, the term *interference* is often used. This term has gained multiple meanings with respect to this proposed interaction as illustrated by its collection of various modifiers, *linguistic interference, psychological interference,* and *educational interference* (Saville and Troike 1971).

Carrow's (1971, 1972) earlier reported work is relevant to this area of transfer. Her measures across languages indicated that English surpassed Spanish for bilingual children studied. Fur-

thermore, English performance in bilinguals was lower than that
of English monolinguals at early ages (three to five years), but
equal to English monolinguals at later ages (six to seven years).
Although these data suggest a possible causal relationship between bilingualism on the initial "rate" of language acquisition,
it is far from conclusive and is contradicted by other findings.

For instance, Evans (1974) reports the comparison of word-
pair discriminations and word imitations in Spanish and English
for monolingual English and bilingual Spanish-English children. Children were asked to discriminate between words containing English sounds considered difficult for Spanish-speakers.
(Examples are the phonemes /b/ and /v/ which are distinct in
English but not as clearly separate in Spanish.) Additionally,
children were requested to imitate a series of words in each
language whose pronunciation made use of various phonological
rules. Bilinguals did not differ from monolinguals on any of these
English tasks. As expected, however, bilinguals scored significantly higher than monolinguals on all Spanish tasks. García
and Trujillo (1979) report a similar finding after they compared
bilingual (Spanish-English) and monolingual (English) three-,
four-, five-, six-, and seven-year-olds on high error-risk phonemes
(phonemes adult Spanish-speakers mispronounce in Spanish),
and simple-to-complex syntactic forms. Bilinguals did not differ
from monolinguals on English imitation tasks (both groups
scored near 100 percent correct) but did differ significantly (made
less errors) on Spanish tasks. This was the case at all age levels.

At present few detailed investigations of bilingual acquisition
have appeared in the literature. Such unavailability of data limits
seriously the types of valid conclusions related to early childhood
bilingualism and questions of acquisition and transfer. The remainder of this chapter presents in some detail an empirical
study which attempts to address this void for Spanish-English
bilingual children.

Bilingual Acquisition in Early Childhood:
An Empirical Study

The following research has attempted to address the various
aspects of bilingualism. It is, first, a description of bilingual
development in that children under study were from bilingual

home environments, and measures were obtained in each language. Secondly, it allows the comparison of bilingual and monolingual children across various linguistic measures. Subsets of children matched by age and Socio-Economic Status (SES) were included in the study. In doing so it attempts to deal with some notions of positive and negative transfer. The availability of home language measures adds an additional dimension insofar as it is related to overall language input and use across the two languages of the bilingual. In summary, the investigation attempts to generate some initial answers to questions of use, input, and transfer which are of special theoretical and applied importance to early childhood bilingualism.

Subjects were participants in one bilingual-bicultural preschool program and several neighboring preschool programs not emphasizing a bilingual-bicultural curriculum. These preschools were located in a section of a moderately sized (population 150,000) city within a predominantly Mexican-American neighborhood. At the time of the study, the Spanish-surnamed population of the city was close to 10 percent, and, of this population, 75 percent of the Spanish-surnamed children attended the five public schools in this neighborhood.

The bilingual preschool was staffed by one early childhood specialist, certified as a preschool instructor, who served as co-ordinator and head teacher. Additionally, each mother served as a teacher on at least one day each week with a minimum of two mothers assuming this role each day. Mothers were also required to spend an additional day, usually on Fridays, developing and preparing curriculum for those days they served as teachers. (Mothers were paid on an hourly basis for each of these staff functions.)

All families of the children involved in the study lived within the designated area indicated above and can be described as economically disadvantaged (as defined by U.S. Department of Labor per-annum family income, 1976). Ages of the children ranged from thirty-six to fifty months; mothers' ages ranged from eighteen to thirty-three years. All participants of the bilingual preschool were made aware of the bilingual-bicultural curriculum effort prior to inclusion in the preschool. It was necessary for each mother to speak both Spanish and English although the ability to speak each language varied individually.

From this population, twelve bilingual children, and one monolingual (Spanish-speaking) child were identified for extensive observation. The criterion used for identification of this group of children was two-fold. First, preentry interviews with the mother included questions which related to the mother's, child's, and family's use of Spanish and English in the home. Secondly, the preschool staff was asked to rate the children's ability in each language given their performance within the preschool setting. Those children whose mothers indicated that both languages were used in the home by the family and specifically indicated that both they and their child spoke (used) both languages at home were considered for inclusion in the longitudinal observations. Children who were given a high rating in use of both languages by the preschool staff and fulfilled the previous requirements were considered bilinguals and included in the longitudinal observations. Sixteen children initially met the requirements; four of these children left the preschool before completion of twelve consecutive monthly observations. Monolingual children whose only home language was English were recruited from neighboring preschool programs. Table 2.1 presents the age in months for all children during their participation in the study.

Collection and Transcription of Language Samples   An eight-by-ten-foot room at the preschool was used to record mother-child interaction. A TEAC 140 cassette recorder was used to record all language interactions. Mother-child interactions were recorded twice each month in each language for bilingual pairs and once each month for monolingual pairs. During the first six months of the study, the mother-child pairs used a standardized free-productive language stimulus item (Educational Testing Service Test: *Circus*, productive test 10C) during each recording session. The picture portrayed a circus scene with several items which could be discussed (animals, clowns, balls, etc.) and which was intended to serve as a catalyst for increased mother-child interaction.

At the beginning of each session the mother was given a set of instructions and then was left in the room with her child. Mothers were requested to carry on a normal conversation with their child and to use the picture as an initiator. (Bilingual mothers were requested to do so in either one language or the other.)

TABLE 2.1

Age of Bilingual and Monolingual Subjects in Months During Their Participation in the Study

Bilinguals

	#1	#2	#3	#4	#5	#6	#7	#8	#9	#10	#11	#12
Age	36–48	37–49	37–49	36–48	35–47	35–47	36–48	38–50	38–50	38–50	38–50	38–50
Sex	M	F	F	M	M	F	F	M	F	M	M	F

Monolinguals

	#13	#14	#15	#16	#17	#18	#19	#20	#21	#22	#23	#24	#25[a]
Age	36–48	37–49	36–48	37–49	37–49	38–50	37–49	37–49	38–50	38–50	38–50	38–50	37–49
Sex	F	M	F	M	M	F	F	M	M	F	F	M	M

[a]Monolingual Spanish Speaker

During the last six months of the study another type of language stimulus was used during the recording session. This stimulus was a three-dimensional playhouse with a number of fixed objects (furniture, people, etc.). Instructions given before the beginning of a session were similar to those used during the previous months of the study. Each session allowed for ten to fifteen minutes of uninterrupted dialogue between mother and child.

Scoring   The analysis of language use of mother and child in English and/or Spanish was conducted by three bilingual graduate students. One student, T^1, transcribed and analyzed all Spanish language sessions. Another student, T^2, transcribed all English sessions. A third graduate student, T^3, transcribed both the Spanish and English language sessions. An utterance was defined following the rules specified by Brown (1973). Only one additional constraint was added: complete imitation (repetition) by either mother or child of a previous utterance was not included in the detailed analysis. This became important because of the very high rate of imitation by bilingual children during Spanish language sessions. (This phenomenon will be discussed later.) It was felt that the treatment of imitated and nonimitated utterances in a separate manner would add qualitatively to the analysis. Reliability of language transcriptions was handled by comparing the language scripts of the two transcribers. (T^3 compared her scripts with those of T^1 and T^2.) Only language transcriptions which were agreed upon 100 percent were included in the pool of utterances analyzed. This 100-percent-agreement criterion led to the elimination of 2–18 percent (range) of utterances per session.

Analysis of Language Samples   The present collection of language samples allows several questions concerning bilingualism and early childhood to be addressed. One important analysis possible was of a longitudinal nature. A minimum of twelve sequential monthly recordings were taken for each bilingual mother-child pair in both Spanish and English. For monolingual mother-child pairs the number of sequential monthly measures was six. Unfortunately, the small and variable number of utterances within each of these separate intervals posed serious problems for a detailed monthly longitudinal analysis. For bilingual children very few Spanish utterances were emitted during each session. The range of Spanish utterances per session was between 2 and 53 with a session mean of 18.32. For English, the range of utterances per session was 11–64 with a session mean of 37.5. Therefore, for both groups of children, it became impossible to make any valid analysis of longitudinal changes on a monthly basis. Previous work has attempted to include at least one hundred utterances at each of several temporal periods (Cazden 1972).

For bilingual children, instead of a precise month-by-month longitudinal analysis, a first-half-to-second-half analysis was completed. For purposes of this analysis, the separate temporally obtained samples for the first six-month recordings were combined and a total of 100 utterances were selected. The selection of utterances was completed so that one-third were from the initial sequence of sessions, one-third from the middle sequence of sessions, and one-third from the terminal sequence of sessions. This same procedure was used to select an additional 100 utterances for the second six months of recordings. This set of 200 utterances, both for mothers and children, were used in the analysis. For monolingual children, only 100 utterances were analyzed in detail. This was done since recordings for these children were taken only for a six-month period.

Of primary interest were several structural and nonstructural dependent measures which have been studied extensively in monolingual children. These included MLU, morphological structures (plural, prepositions, contractions, copula, articles), gender and number agreement, vocabulary (number and typed token sets), in addition to several other qualitative comparisons (negative syntactic constructions, imitation, and use of nonspecific nouns). The following is a description of these language measures:

Mean Length of Utterance (MLU)   This measure has been proposed as a relatively standard assessment of language development in children (Snow 1972; Brown 1973). This measure has as an index the number of morphemes per utterance, where an utterance is a unit of speech demarcated prosodically and by pauses (Brown 1973). MLU for English language samples was calculated in this manner. For Spanish language samples, these same considerations were also used as the basic guide. One major problem with this measure when comparing between Spanish and English is the idiosyncratic morpheme structures within each language. For instance the utterance "la muchacha" would receive a score of three given the morpheme guide because the article "la" must agree in gender and number with the noun "muchacha." This is not the case for English translation of the utterance, "the girl," which would receive a score of two. Because of several of these inequalities it is not appropriate to compare directly the presently calculated English MLU to Spanish MLU although some rough comparisons may heuristically be of benefit. (Appendixes 2.1 and 2.2 present the rules used for MLU computations for English and Spanish, respectively.)

Plurals   The use and construction of the plural morpheme is similar in each language (an addition of the inflection *s* or *es*). The use of obligatory plurals was assessed in each language. (Obligation was determined by the previous statements of the mother. Example: "What are these," calls for a plural response by the child.)

Prepositions   The correct use of prepositions in each language was important due to the varied use of translated prepositional labels across Spanish and English. For instance, *in* (English) and *en* (Spanish) are directly translatable in some cases and not in others. (*En* has approximately eight possible meanings in Spanish; this is not the case for the English *in*.) (Stockwell, Bowen, and Martin 1965.) Appropriate use of the following prepositions was observed: English—*in, on, for, with;* Spanish—*en, por, para, de, con.*

Contractions   These forms exist only in English and only rarely in Spanish. (Specific contractions observed: Can't, don't, I'm, they're.)

Copula   In English, correct use of the verb *to be* was of interest due its contrast in Spanish. In Spanish, two possibilities—*ser* (permanent status) and *estar* (temporary status)—were assessed.

Articles   For English the correct use of articles (a, an, the) was assessed. For Spanish, the use of articles with respect to gender agreement (el, la, un, una) and number agreement (el, los; la, las; una, unas; uno, unos) was evaluated.

Demonstrative Pronouns   Of interest was the obligatory agreement inherent in each language. In English, agreement with respect to number is obligatory (this, these; that, those). In Spanish, both gender and number agreement is necessary (este, esta, estos, estas; esa, ese, esos, esas).

Use of "Se" for unspecified agent   This is a particular characteristic of Spanish. It was of interest due to its morphological complexity and the absence of a parallel form in English.

Vocabulary   A vocabulary score was derived for each child based on the number of different lexical items recorded within the utterances analyzed.

Type-Token Ratio   An additional vocabulary diversity computation took into consideration the repetition factor in the child's dialogue. "Type" refers to vocabulary items; and "Token" refers to occurrences of any item. As this ratio approaches 1.0, an increase in vocabulary diversity is indicated. This measure was calculated on the first 100 vocabulary items recorded within each 100 utterances analyzed for each child in the study.

Negative Syntactic Construction   In English, negative construction calls for the insertion of *no* or *not* after a designated auxiliary verb form ("I do *not* want"). In Spanish, *no* is inserted prior to the verb form ("Yo *no* quiero"). Therefore, this measure allowed an analysis of structurally different syntagmatic forms across the languages of the bilingual children.

Imitation   Exact utterance repetitions of the mother's preceding utterance by the child were treated separately from "spontaneous" (nonrepeated) utterances for purposes of analysis. A percentage of imitation was calculated from those sessions from which the 100 percent "spontaneous" utterances analyzed were selected. This measure was calculated for each session by dividing the number of imitated utterances by the total number of utterances and multiplying by 100.

Nonspecific Nouns   Recently, Brown (1977) has suggested an alternative measure for gauging the complexity of a spontaneous utterance. It is a simple cognitive index dealing with nouns only. It divides them into two classes: specific—The child speaker had something specific in mind as a referent; nonspecific—The child speaker had in mind a nonspecific instance of a set, some nonspecific set of instances, all of a general class, any abstraction (time, idea, etc.), or any metalinguistic meaning (e.g., the word *name*). Excluded were numerals, letters, greetings, and formulas (e.g., "wait a minute"). The technique, although narrowly focusing on nouns, avoids the problem of idiosyncratic language (or dialect) differences in morphology and syntax across languages. Its emphasis on the semantic quality of an utterance may be a more useful base for a comparative analysis of language acquisition between the two languages of the bilingual.

Language Use in the Home   During four months (months three, six, nine, and twelve) of the study, observations of Spanish and English use were also conducted in the home of each of the bilingual children. During these sessions an outside observer, herself bilingual, visited the home sometime after school and before the evening meal. The observer remained in the home for one hour during each visit but officially recorded speech use only during the last half hour. The observer coded the use of Spanish and/or English within ten-second time intervals. Any recognizable Spanish or English word or combination of words sufficed to indicate language use. (Excluded were proper nouns, "oh," "ah," and the word *no*.) Present during these observations were the child, the child's mother, and at least one older sibling. Each bilingual child of the study had at least one older sibling, and one or more younger siblings, and two children had more than one older sibling. The range for older siblings was six to nine years of age. The observer further coded the initiator and the intended receiver of the utterance. The observer seated herself at a distance from the child under observation and followed that child throughout the house if necessary. (A conscious attempt was made to have the observer remain unobtrusive by minimizing the physical movement, physical proximity, and verbal involvement.) At no time did the observer leave the confines of the home during these visits for observation. During one of these visits to each subject's home, a second observer was present to assess interobserver agreement. Each observer coded language use using the same procedures, but independent from each other. Percentage of agreement was calculated for each form of coded interaction (Spanish: mother to child, child to mother, sibling to child, child to sibling). Interobserver agreement ranged between 83 and 97 percent, with a mean of 86.2 percent, for each type of coded interaction during these visits.

The Spanish and English of the Bilingual   A comparison between the languages of the bilingual subjects is presented in Tables 2.2, 2.3, and 2.4. For each subject, Spanish and English measures of MLU, vocabulary count, type-token ratio, percentage of nonspecific nouns, and percentage of imitated utterances are presented. The absolute number of identified plurals, articles, prepositions, and conjunctions are also presented. Each of these measures is presented for the first six months and the second six months of the study. An inspection of these dependent measures for each language longitudinally suggests little, if any, developmental trend. That is, measures taken during the first six months of the study, when compared to those of the second six months, reveal no significant increases or decreases. Although slight increases or decreases are apparent for several subjects, no consistent pattern emerges.

Although developmental changes were not observed, these measures indicate some level of language production in each language for all children. In almost all cases, these measures indicate a more "advanced" use of English than Spanish. Although English and Spanish MLU are not directly comparable due to differential calculation formulas, a consistently higher English MLU score resulted for all subjects except S_1. At this level of acquisition it seems reasonable to suggest that Spanish MLU may be "inflated" with respect to English MLU due to article-noun obligatory agreements (both in number and gender) in Spanish that do not exist in English. Yet, English MLU was higher for each of these subjects—nearly 2.00 units for each subject.

TABLE 2.2

A Comparison of Spanish and English by Selected Linguistic Measures for Bilingual Subjects of the Study for the First Nine Months (a), and Second Nine Months (b) of the Study

		Subjects							
		#1		#2		#3		#4	
		Span.	Eng.	Span.	Eng.	Span.	Eng.	Span.	Eng.
MLU	(a)	2.38	1.95	1.55	3.36	1.66	3.56	1.62	3.59
	(b)	2.48	2.38	1.67	3.49	1.73	3.79	1.61	3.71
Vocabulary	(a)	77	50	50	100	38	110	49	120
	(b)	81	73	63	98	41	117	59	116
Type/Token	(a)	.50	.26	.43	.55	.37	.51	.41	.47
	(b)	.51	.38	.35	.59	.41	.56	.38	.56
% Nonspecific	(a)	3	1	2	41	2	14	2	12
Nouns	(b)	8	9	4	38	6	19	2	26
% Imitated	(a)	45	38	52	14	51	7	53	15
Utterances	(b)	31	31	41	3	38	11	42	0
Plurals	(a)	5	10	12	9	7	12	9	9
	(b)	5	7	7	11	12	14	11	4
Articles	(a)	24	16	7	21	9	14	9	24
	(b)	19	19	11	13	6	17	12	17
Prepositions	(a)	1	4	2	16	1	11	2	6
	(b)	6	5	2	12	6	9	4	11
Conjunctions	(a)	1	1	0	7	2	0	1	11
	(b)	3	7	3	14	4	2	3	17

These differences were also apparent in other measures. Vocabulary count and type-token ratio favored English. The percentage of nonspecific nouns in each language also suggests more weighted development in English. For each subject, the percentage of nonspecific nouns was higher in English. The percentage of imitated utterances was high in Spanish, and almost nonexistent in English. This high frequency of imitation has been correlated previously with low MLU in children's acquisition of a single native language (Bloom, Hood, and Lightbrown 1974).

TABLE 2.3

A Comparison of Spanish and English by Selected Linguistic Measures for Bilingual Subjects of the Study for the First Nine Months (a), and Second Nine Months (b) of the Study

		Subjects							
		#5		#6		#7		#8	
		Span.	Eng.	Span.	Eng.	Span.	Eng.	Span.	Eng.
MLU	(a)	1.75	3.61	1.81	3.71	1.48	3.77	1.71	4.01
	(b)	1.63	3.84	1.96	3.62	1.55	4.16	1.83	3.94
Vocabulary	(a)	46	96	73	120	56	89	48	98
	(b)	42	109	79	131	50	112	61	93
Type/Token	(a)	.38	.61	.31	.51	.39	.50	.36	.48
	(b)	.35	.52	.39	.53	.31	.53	0	0
% Nonspecific Nouns	(a)	4	33	6	18	0	21	4	36
	(b)	2	39	7	14	1	17	11	39
% Imitated Utterances	(a)	38	6	29	0	42	14	38	4
	(b)	21	6	27	1	19	4	27	3
Plurals	(a)	10	8	6	7	7	4	6	9
	(b)	7	11	5	11	5	4	11	8
Articles	(a)	9	10	11	7	9	18	13	16
	(b)	12	14	15	12	11	12	11	19
Prepositions	(a)	4	12	6	11	4	6	4	11
	(b)	4	11	14	18	7	9	6	14
Conjunctions	(a)	1	6	0	4	3	11	4	11
	(b)	5	9	2	3	9	14	3	16

Subject 1 stands out as substantially different from the previously described subjects. On each of the measures in which other subjects differed across languages, this subject did not differ. Measures of MLU, vocabulary count, type-token ratio, percentage of specific nouns, percentage of imitated utterances indicated near-equal performance in Spanish. It is important to note that this subject scored much lower on these measures in English than did the other subjects although Spanish measures were higher.

In summary, these data indicate that on the linguistic mea-

TABLE 2.4

A Comparison of Spanish and English by Selected Linguistic Measures for Bilingual Subjects of the Study for the First Nine Months (a), and Second Nine Months (b) of the Study

| | | Subjects | | | | | | | |
| | | #9 | | #10 | | #11 | | #12 | |
		Span.	Eng.	Span.	Eng.	Span.	Eng.	Span.	Eng.
MLU	(a)	1.96	4.03	1.56	4.18	1.71	4.40	1.38	4.49
	(b)	1.93	3.96	1.61	4.09	1.65	4.21	1.56	4.21
Vocabulary	(a)	70	109	62	121	61	114	46	131
	(b)	65	126	54	118	53	131	53	138
Type/Token	(a)	.40	.43	.31	.47	.42	.46	.41	.51
	(b)	.40	.51	0	0	.38	.43	.50	.47
% Nonspecific Nouns	(a)	1	20	3	27	6	17	0	19
	(b)	1	21	4	31	4	25	5	26
% Imitated Utterances	(a)	35	1	27	0	31	0	36	1
	(b)	31	0	19	0	25	0	33	0
Plurals	(a)	5	11	7	14	6	18	5	7
	(b)	7	9	5	10	9	14	5	11
Articles	(a)	12	15	16	21	7	28	11	19
	(b)	16	21	14	9	16	21	13	17
Prepositions	(a)	17	6	3	14	8	14	0	5
	(b)	11	21	7	12	8	19	2	9
Conjunctions	(a)	0	1	0	9	4	14	1	9
	(b)	1	7	1	14	7	9	3	5

sures utilized here, eleven of twelve subjects were substantially advanced in English as compared to Spanish. One subject was nearly equal in each language, but was substantially lower than his bilingual age peers in English and somewhat higher in Spanish than these same peers.

Were these children actually bilingual? Of considerable importance in assessing such a question was the functioning level of these bilinguals on several morphological and syntactic classes which differ between languages. At this level of development, gender and number agreement for article-noun constructions obligatory in nature in Spanish but not in English were of specific interest. The gender agreement required for demonstrative pronouns in Spanish, not required in English, was of corollary interest, as was the number agreement of demonstrative pronouns of necessity in both languages. Also of interest were the negative syntactic constructions in each language. (In Spanish, negative constructions differ from those in English by the placement of the "negative" agent.) It was interesting to compare the use of the *se* for unspecified agent(s) in Spanish, a structural feature not found in English. The appropriate use of the copula was another valuable comparison. In Spanish, copula mastery requires the use of two semantically differentiated verbs: *ser* and *estar*. (Table 2.5 presents each of the above linguistic categories for each language with specific examples provided.)

Table 2.6 presents the results of these comparisons for bilingual subjects. It presents both the total number of observed instances and the percentage correct of the linguistic features of interest in either (or both) Spanish and English. With respect to gender agreement, subjects indicated near perfect (100 percent) correct obligatory agreement for both article-noun productions and demonstrative pronoun-noun production. High obligatory agreement was also indicated for article-noun productions in Spanish and demonstrative pronoun productions in both Spanish and English. *Se* in Spanish to indicate unspecified agent(s) was used infrequently but always correctly. Negative constructions were observed more in English than Spanish, but in all cases were also used correctly in each language.

Copula constructions were of special interest in Spanish due to the two separate morphemes (*ser* and *estar*) available in Spanish. Although the use of *ser* was more common than *estar*, correct use of each was high (90 percent for *ser*, 100 percent for *estar*). In addition, correct use of the English copula was observed at the same high level (91 percent).

The main purpose of those comparisons presented in Table 6 and discussed above has been to substantiate the bilinguality of the subjects. Although MLU was consistently low in Spanish and general production levels were low in Spanish, these children did show the ability to handle complex forms of Spanish morphology and syntax. In those areas of structure where the languages differ either by nonexistence of particular structures or

TABLE 2.5

Comparative Analysis of Linguistic Features in Each Language

Spanish	English

1. Gender Agreement
   (a) articles (el, un, la, una) (el muchacho, la muchacha)
   (b) demonstrative pronouns (este, esta) (este muchacho, esta muchacha)
	Gender Agreement:
	(a) none required
	
	(b) none required

2. Number Agreement:
   (a) articles (los, las) (el pato, los patos)
   (b) demonstrative pronouns (este, estos) (este muchacho, estos muchachos)
	Number Agreement:
	(a) none required
	
	(b) demonstrative pronouns (this, these; that, those)

3. Use of *se* for unspecified agent(s) (*se* quebro)	nonexistent
4. Negative Construction: (Yo *no* quiero)	Negative Construction: (I do *not* want)

5. Copula:
   (a) ser (permanent status)
   (b) estar (temporary status)
	Copula:
	(a) to be

differential structural forms, children handled these inconsistencies between the languages quite well, with very few errors. This conclusion is important since it is an independent indicator that these children exemplified a complex level of bilingual functioning.

The English of the Bilinguals and Monolinguals   Considering that the bilingual children of the study were characterized by more than simple functioning capabilities in Spanish, the intriguing comparison between these children's English language development and that of monolingual English children is of both theoretical and applied importance. The notion of negative transfer within these bilingual children, at a general level, might

TABLE 2.6

Percentage of Correct and Total Number of Selected Spanish and English Linguistic Measures for Bilingual Children

		Gender Agreement		Number Agreement			Copula			
		Article– Noun	Demonstrative Pronoun–Noun	Article– Noun	Demonstrative Pronoun–Noun	Se	to be	ser	estar	Negative Construction
Spanish	%	91[a]	100	95	100	100		93	100	100
	No.	271	58	271	58	26		83	23	31
English	%				100		91			88
	No.				48		111			131

[a] Of the errors identified, more were Spanish nonagreement errors (*un* instead of *una*) and few were English substitution errors (*a* instead of *un*).

TABLE 2.7

A Comparison of Bilingual (Spanish/English) and Monolingual (English) Children Matched for English MLU on Selected English Linguistic Measures

	#1	#13	#2	#14	#3	#15	#4	#16
				Subjects				
MLU	1.95	1.88	3.36	3.34	3.56	3.58	3.59	3.59
Vocabulary	50	60	100	129	110	102	120	130
Type/Token	.26	.45	.55	.54	.51	.50	.47	.56
% Nonspecific Nouns	1	4	41	26	14	7	12	26
% Imitated Utterances	38	34	14	5	7	11	15	18
Plurals	10	10	9	7	12	6	9	8
Articles	16	1	21	18	14	11	24	28
Prepositions	4	0	16	6	11	8	6	20
Conjunctions	1	0	7	0	0	4	11	20
Contractions	6	9	14	20	24	16	36	14

predict delayed English development. At a more specific level, examination of lexical, morphological, and syntactic features in English might prove valuable in evaluating more thoroughly the occurrence of both positive and negative transfer.

Tables 2.7, 2.8, and 2.9 present a comparison of bilingual and monolingual children matched (as closely as possible) on English MLU for selected linguistic features in English. Subjects 1 and 13 obtained relatively low MLU scores (1.95 and 1.88 respectively). All other subjects' MLU scores were noticeably higher (3.36–4.81). Even with the earliest research using MLU as an indicator of developmental language change (Cazden 1972), its idiosyncratic nature in children has been recognized. These idiosyncracies were noted with these children. For this reason subjects were matched on MLU in an attempt to compare English performance with other linguistic indices.

When such a comparison is made of matched pairs, it is difficult to ascertain any systematic difference. For vocabulary count, monolinguals seem to demonstrate a somewhat greater degree

TABLE 2.8

A Comparison of Bilingual (Spanish/English) and Monolingual (English) Children Matched for English MLU on Selected English Linguistic Measures

	Subjects							
	#5	#17	#6	#18	#7	#19	#8	#20
MLU	3.61	3.65	3.71	3.68	3.77	3.85	4.01	3.96
Vocabulary	96	116	120	117	89	119	98	130
Type/Token	.61	.52	.51	.41	.50	.56	.48	.43
% Nonspecific Nouns	33	28	18	27	21	26	36	19
% Imitated Utterances	6	3	0	2	14	6	4	0
Plurals	8	16	7	6	4	11	9	5
Articles	10	7	7	14	18	16	16	13
Prepositions	12	14	11	9	6	7	11	6
Conjunctions	6	9	4	8	11	5	11	15
Contractions	14	11	12	6	17	8	15	7

of vocabulary diversity. Although this is consistent, differences are very small. The type-token ratio provides another measure of vocabulary diversity. Differences are almost nonexistent between matched pairs, although there does seem to be an increase in this diversity measure as MLU increases. Similar results are evident for the use of nonspecific nouns. Recall that this measure attempts to identify lexical use of specificity and abstractness. No major systematic difference is evident for the matched pairs. But, as MLU increases for these pairs, relative use of nonspecific nouns increases. The imitation of mother utterances also follows this same pattern. Differences between matched pairs on this measure were very small. Yet, for the low MLU subjects this measure was much higher (34 percent and 38 percent for S_1 and S_{13}, respectively) than for the remaining high MLU subjects (range of 5–18 percent). A review of matched pair comparisons of bilingual and monolingual subjects on the remainder of the morpheme measures in Tables 2.7, 2.8, and 2.9 indicated the absence of any systematic differences.

TABLE 2.9

A Comparison of Bilingual (Spanish/English) and Monolingual (English) Children Matched for English MLU on Selected English Linguistic Measures

	Subjects							
	#9	#21	#10	#22	#11	#23	#12	#24
MLU	4.03	4.10	4.18	4.28	4.40	4.45	4.49	4.81
Vocabulary	109	113	121	131	114	131	131	129
Type/Token	.43	.51	.47	.54	.46	.52	.51	.45
% Nonspecific Nouns	20	18	27	31	17	25	19	26
% Imitated Utterances	1	0	0	3	0	0	1	0
Plurals	11	16	14	11	18	11	7	9
Articles	15	21	21	16	28	23	19	29
Prepositions	6	2	14	11	8	16	5	8
Conjunctions	1	11	9	4	4	6	9	6
Contractions	6	7	17	26	17	21	9	15

Chi-square comparisons on the absolute number of plurals, articles, prepositions, conjunctions, and contractions were performed for bilingual and monolingual English subjects. Except for those comparisons involving Subjects 1 and 13, no significant differences were found on these measures. For those comparisons involving these two subjects with other subjects, all subjects scored significantly higher on these measures. (Recall that these two subjects were lowest in English MLU; see Table 7.)

Only a tentative comparison of Spanish among bilinguals and monolinguals was possible due to the inclusion of a single monolingual Spanish-speaker in the study. Table 2.10 presents a comparison of representative subjects and the monolingual speaker on the same Spanish linguistic measures identified earlier. Although all subjects were approximately the same age, each of the bilingual's Spanish MLU is much lower than that of the Spanish monolingual (differences range from 1.62 to 2.56). With respect to vocabulary, the monolingual speaker produced a higher

TABLE 2.10

A Comparison of Spanish Measures for Four Representative Bilingual (Spanish/English) Subjects and a Monolingual (Spanish) Subject

	Subjects				
	Bilingual (Spanish/English)				Monolingual (Spanish)
	#1	#2	#3	#4	#25
Age (mo.)	40	43	43	42	43
MLU	2.48	1.67	1.73	1.61	4.00
Vocabulary	81	63	41	59	93
Type/Token	.51	.35	.41	.41	.57
% Nonspecific Nouns	8	4	6	2	21
% Imitated Utterances	31	41	38	42	1
Plurals	5	7	12	11	14
Articles	19	11	6	12	34
Prepositions	6	2	6	4	19
Conjunctions	3	3	4	3	14

total of different lexical items and scored higher on the vocabulary diversity measure (type-token ratio). Yet, it was clear that the bilingual subjects did demonstrate a substantial vocabulary count. The increased use of nonspecific nouns is weighted in the direction of high MLU. That is, as MLU increased in Spanish, the percentage of nonspecific nouns also increased. The monolingual child scored highest with respect to this measure. The most striking difference between the bilingual and monolingual subjects was observed in the percentage of imitated utterances. For bilinguals, this ranged between 31 and 52 percent while for the monolingual Spanish subject it was 1 percent.

With respect to particular morphological classes, little difference was apparent in the plural and article category. Bilinguals' use of these forms was lower in absolute number but still reliably observable in each child. The number of prepositions and conjunctions for bilinguals differed substantially from that of the monolingual. (For bilinguals, two to six prepositions were observed; nineteen were observed in the monolingual. The range of conjunctions observed in bilinguals was three to four while a total of fourteen were observed in the speech of the monolingual.)

Home Language   Analysis of bilingualism (and language in general) must attempt to incorporate naturalistic observations of language use so as to investigate more fully the phenomena. In the present study, it was not possible to obtain an utterance-by-utterance account of home language. But, home observation did allow one level of language-use information. Of particular interest was the use of Spanish, English, and mixed Spanish-English utterances by the subjects, their mothers, and their older siblings during after-school, home interactions. This level of information constitutes only a very gross measure of qualitative linguistic input and social norms of linguistic interaction. Yet, it does give some impression of the Spanish, English, or mixed-language models which were present in the child's home environment.

Table 2.11 presents the percentage of ten-second intervals in which Spanish, English, or mixed utterances were directed by the mothers or older siblings to the subjects and vice versa. (Each ten-second interval was coded for the occurrence of an English, Spanish, or both for the subject, mother, and sibling. In addition, the direction of the coded utterance was indicated if the utterance was initiated by the subject or directed to the subject by the mother or sibling.) In general, mother speech directed to the subject was predominantly in Spanish (a range of 65–89 percent of the intervals were coded as Spanish across the twelve mothers). Spanish and English directed from subjects to mothers was fairly evenly distributed. For mother-child speech interaction, few intervals were coded for mixed utterances (a range of 1–15 percent).

For subject-to-sibling and sibling-to-subject speech, English was the predominant language used. The intervals coded as English-only ranged between 70 and 90 percent while Spanish-only ranged between 8 and 29 percent. Almost no (0–5 percent) in-

TABLE 2.11

Percentage of 10-second intervals in which Spanish, English, and Spanish-English mixed utterances were directed by the mother or older sibling to the subject, and percentage of intervals in which Spanish, English, and Spanish-English mixed utterances were directed by the subject to the mother or older sibling. (Percentage occurrence is calculated by considering the total number of intervals in which some language use was observed.)

	Mother-to-Subject			Subject-to-Mother			Sibling-to-Subject			Subject-to-Sibling		
	Spanish	English	Spanish & English	Spanish	English	Spanish & English	Spanish	English	Spanish & English	Spanish	English	Spanish & English
S_1	85	12	3	82	17	1	55	41	4	38	61	1
S_2	81	14	5	73	26	1	37	57	6	27	73	0
S_3	82	17	1	70	29	1	36	61	3	19	81	0
S_4	89	10	1	52	43	5	20	73	7	34	66	0
S_5	73	14	13	69	29	2	27	70	3	32	67	1
S_6	82	6	12	71	26	3	32	61	7	39	61	0
S_7	86	11	3	63	36	1	43	55	2	40	57	3
S_8	71	18	11	69	27	4	35	62	3	26	72	2
S_9	69	29	3	73	26	1	26	71	3	29	70	1
S_{10}	73	16	14	71	23	6	22	73	5	29	71	0
S_{11}	77	9	14	65	35	0	25	69	6	28	68	4
S_{12}	75	23	2	63	37	0	20	77	3	23	74	3
$\overline{X}$	78.58	14.92	6.83	68.41	29.50	2.08	31.50	64.17	4.33	30.33	68.42	1.17

tervals were coded as having mixed-language utterances for speech directed to subjects by siblings or vice versa.

Several conclusions can be drawn from this data: subjects' use of Spanish and English in the home was indeed occurring; although this was the case, Spanish was confined to child-mother speech exchange; English was predominant in subject-sibling speech exchange; and mixed utterances were almost entirely absent from the coded speech, with its occurrence primarily confined to mother's speech directed to the subject.

General Discussion   The present study has focused on the speech of young children and their mothers, in this particular case, children from either bilingual (Spanish and English) or monolingual (English) home environments. Children's utterances were selected from mother-child discourse and subjected primarily to a structural analysis. A comparison of Spanish and English features of these utterances was conducted for the bilingual children of the study. Additionally, comparisons of bilinguals' Spanish and English to monolingual speakers of each of these languages were also conducted.

Valid conclusions concerning linguistic competence based only on counts of morphemes are most hazardous because single-context, data collection is often employed; data discussed here were gathered in similar (somewhat standard) speech-elicitation environments in both Spanish and English. Yet, some tentative conclusions seem warranted. For eleven of twelve bilingual children, Spanish-English comparisons across a wide range of dependent measures indicated a much higher level of performance in English than in Spanish. Since MLU is not a useful comparative measure across languages due to the inherent differences in its calculation between Spanish and English, measures on other linguistic parameters seem more appropriate for comparative analyses. These include vocabulary, nonspecific noun, and imitation measures. On these measures distinct English "weighting" is most obvious. The children tended to produce twice as many different vocabulary items in English than in Spanish; nonspecific-noun use in relation to specific-noun use was consistently higher for all children in English, and the percentage of utterances imitated from the mother was many times higher in Spanish than English. Each of these characteristics in Spanish is similar to characteristics of monolingual children at initial levels of language development (Brown 1973).

Yet, it would be a mistake to conclude that these same children were not competent Spanish-speakers at other than the most basic levels. An analysis of number and gender agreement features of Spanish as they relate to article-noun and demonstrative-pronoun-noun utterances indicated otherwise. That is, these children demonstrated few errors in these obligatory contexts. Analysis of linguistic features which were nonexistent in English but available in Spanish (use of *se* for unspecified agent(s), and the multiple copula of *ser* and *estar*) as well as the correct formulation of negative constructions (which required different juxtapositioning of negative agents in Spanish and English) added still further evidence of "sophisticated" structural functioning in Spanish by these subjects.

Therefore, for these bilingual subjects, a clear performance weight in favor of English was observed, although analysis of Spanish utterances indicated a more than a basic use of Spanish. The twelfth bilingual child of the study (S_1) was more clearly bilingual in that linguistic measures used in this study were near equal in both languages. (It was the case that this subject was more characteristic of a low-level English speaker in MLU, vocabulary, imitation, and nonspecific measures than the other bilingual children on these same measures.)

When bilingual children were compared to monolingual speakers, Spanish performance was clearly much lower. In this form of comparison, MLU is an appropriate comparative tool, and, for each bilingual child Spanish MLU was 50 percent lower than that for the monolingual Spanish child. (Recall that all of these children were approximately the same age.) A comparison of matched MLU pairs with children in English indicated very little systematic difference between bilinguals and monolinguals for combined counts of specific morpheme categories. A significant matched-pair difference resulted for only subjects 1 and 13. These subjects were lower in English MLU (1.95 and 1.88, respectively). All other subjects at MLU levels equal to or greater than 3.36, when compared to each other, did not differ on the productions of the five morpheme categories in English. These results suggest that at a general level there was no apparent negative transfer (or retardation) effect for English as a result of the bilingual character of the children. It is possible that unequally weighted bilinguals like the ones of this study, which indicated a disparity between English and Spanish (with English performance noticeably higher than Spanish), would not be likely candidates for negative transfer. Yet, these children were quite capable of conforming to morphological and syntactic rules of the Spanish language. Although this is only an unsubstantiated guess, I would be inclined to think the bilingual nature of these children characterizes a very large segment of children who have been and will be labeled Spanish-English "bilinguals" in this country.

The additional observation of the bilingual children's home environment adds a further dimension to the extrapolation of the mother-child interaction data. In the home, Spanish and English directed toward the subjects seemed to vary between mothers' speech to subjects (Spanish) and siblings' speech to subjects (English). This same division occurred for the subjects' own speech to either mother (Spanish) or siblings (English). Although these boundaries did exist, it was clear that the child's speech environment at home did consist of both languages. In addition, the child did emit a relatively large sample of both Spanish and English utterances.

Since no detailed qualitative analysis of these data was possible, it remains unclear how these utterances were similar to or different from those observed during the recorded mother-child interaction sessions at the preschool (and which have undergone detailed analysis here). It does seem appropriate to conclude that these children were exposed to two languages at home but that the focus of exposure for Spanish differed from that for English. These boundaries seem similar to those reported by sociolinguists who have attempted to map Spanish and English use outside of the home setting. Fishman and his colleagues (1971) have documented some of these neighborhood boundaries for urban Puerto Rican populations. In this study, boundaries were observed within the home and related to particular social interactions and not physically confined to particular areas of the home. Further analysis of this type adds significantly to our understanding of such separations of language and their influence on acquisition and use.

Of continued interest in the study of bilingualism has been the interactive influences of the two languages (traditionally labeled "interference" or transfer). Some analysis of transfer was possible by contrasting the use of specific morphological classes between the two languages. For instance, some indication of negative transfer might be substantiated by the children's errors of Spanish morphemes which exist in English but are structurally dissimilar. This might be the case for the use of the Spanish copula, *ser* and *estar*. (In English only the copula *to be* is available for use.) Yet, bilinguals had little trouble with the separate use of *ser*, although *estar* was used infrequently. Additionally, these same children had a little trouble with the use of English copula (see Table 2.6). Another possible instance of negative transfer owing to differences in surface structure across languages may be located in the construction of negative statements. (In English *no* or *not* is placed after the verb form; in Spanish *no* is placed before the verb form.) Again, few errors in handling these two different formulations were observed in the bilingual children (Table 2.6).

Of course, positive transfer across linguistic modes must also be considered. It is very difficult to make a strong case for its occurrence in this study owing to the individual differences which were apparent. Yet, several cautious remarks may serve to indicate its possible occurrence. For instance, Subject 1 produced a very high incidence of articles in English compared to his English MLU matched monolingual subject (sixteen for S_1 and 1 for S_{13}). Article use in Spanish requires substantially more obligatory considerations than article use in English. A further possible indication of positive transfer is the near equally correct occurrence of pluralization for bilinguals in both languages and monolinguals in English. (Plurals are formed in similar ways in both languages.) In any case, it seems likely that such comparisons of performance across structurally similar classes of morphemes may be indications of positive transfer, just as analysis of errors across structurally dissimilar classes may serve as indications of negative transfer.

Up to this point, I have been concerned with particular analyses and conclusions which interest those researchers studying bilingualism. Yet, studies which involve bilingual acquisition must be viewed from two perspectives: how do these studies reflect specific information of multilingual acquisition with respect to the languages studied, and how do these studies reflect a subset of research which is directed at understanding the general phenomena of language acquisition? Therefore, studies of bilingual acquisition provide important information specific to subsets of a language population as well as information relevant to language acquisition in general. Investigators active in bilingual research must be willing to deal with each of these issues if they are to maximize the analysis which they perform. For instance, Slobin (1971) has recommended the study of bilingual acquisition so as to investigate the theoretical notions of language universals. He suggests that linguistic features first to appear in bilinguals might empirically verify specific theoretical predictions of universals as well as simple versus complex structural features. Although Padilla and Liebman (1975) point out particular problems with this line of logic, especially the assumption of equal language input (access), some analysis along these lines may prove beneficial.

In this study, lack of equal performance in the languages of the bilingual raises some issues with respect to language acquisition in general. The home data indicated quite clearly that the children were exposed to substantial amounts of Spanish and English from both their mothers and siblings, although this exposure was weighted in Spanish for mothers and in English for siblings. But, in the detailed analysis of mother-child interaction (recorded at the preschool) eleven of the twelve bilingual children performed at much higher levels in English than in Spanish. The twelfth subject was nearly equal in both but much lower than the other subjects in English. The fact that English was much higher than Spanish, although general exposure to Spanish in the home was substantial, indicates two possible conclusions.

First, it is possible that the "contexts" of the mother-child interaction as recorded at the preschool somehow limited a measure of language competence in Spanish. That is, since these interactions took place at the preschool, Spanish performance in this setting was diminished due to its social association with the social rule: "In school speak English not Spanish." Although this may have been operating, it is likely that its influence was minimized by the bilingual nature of the preschool and the customary presence of the mother in that setting. Yet, it is still very possible, since other data indicate "rules" such as these are prevalent (Edelman 1969).

Secondly, if one assumes that the "contextual" influence discussed above is minimal, variables other than exposure to the language must be operating in order to account for the differences observed between Spanish and English performance. In essence, some sort of selective influence with respect to language acquisition must be operative. Brown (1973) suggests that in considering important influences during language acquisition, social variables do not account for the major improvement or change in a child's language. They do not "impel" children to speak like adults (Cazden and Brown 1975). In the present study, this alternative explanation cannot be excluded. Other studies of bilingualism have also indicated the importance of social interaction variables (Gardner and Lambert 1972), but the influence of such variables has been associated with use, not acquisition. Given the level of the present subjects' language, the role of socially identifiable variables in the acquisition process must also be considered. Therefore, the study of bilingualism, especially those studies directed at acquisition data which demonstrate unequal language acquisition, may shed some very interesting light on potential variables of importance during language acquisition in general.

References

Bloom, L., Hood, L., Lightbrown, P. 1974. Imitation in language development: If, when and why. *Cognitive Psychology* 6: 380–420.

Bowerman, M. 1975. Crosslinguistic similarities at two stages of syntactic development. In *Foundations of language development*, eds., E. Lenneberg and E. Lenneberg, pp. 267–82. London: UNESCO Press.

Braine, M. D. S. 1976. *Children's first word combinations.* Monographs of the Society for Research in child development.

Brown, R. 1973. *A first language: The early stages.* Cambridge, Mass.: Harvard University Press.

Brown, R. 1977. Psycholinguistic Review. Paper presented at meeting of the Eastern Psychological Association, Boston, Mass., April.

Carrow, E. 1971. Comprehension of English and Spanish by preschool Mexican-American children. *Modern Language Journal* 55: 299–307.

Carrow, E. 1972. Auditory comprehension of English by monolingual and bilingual preschool children. *Journal of Speech and Hearing Research* 15: 407–12.

Cazden, C. B. 1972. *Child language and education.* New York: Holt, Rinehart and Winston.

Cazden, C., and Brown, R. 1975. The early development of the mother tongue. In *Foundations of language development,* eds. E. Lenneberg and E. Lenneberg, pp. 299–310. London: UNESCO Press.

DeVilliers, J., and DeVilliers, P. 1978. *Language acquisition.* Cambridge, Mass.: Harvard University Press.

Edelman, M. 1969. The contextualization of school children's bilingualism. *Modern Language Journal* 53: 179–82.

Evans, J. S. 1974. Word-pair discrimination and imitation abilities of preschool Spanish-speaking children. *Journal of Learning Disabilities* 7: 573–80.

Fishman, J. 1971. *Bilingualism in the barrio.* New York: Yeshiva University Press, 1971.

García, E., and Trujillo, A. 1979. A developmental comparison of English and Spanish imitation between bilingual and monolingual children. *Journal of Educational Psychology* 21: 161–68.

Gardner, R. C., and Lambert, W. E. 1972. *Attitudes and motivation in second language learning.* Rowley, Mass.: Newbury House.

Geissler, H. 1938. *Zwiesprachiq keit deutscher kinder in Ausland.* Stuttgart: Kohlhammer.

González, G. 1970. The acquisition of Spanish grammar by native Spanish speakers. Ph.D. dissertation, University of Texas at Austin.

Haugen, E. 1972. *The ecology of language.* Stanford, Calif.: Stanford University Press.

Lenneberg, E. H., and Lenneberg, E. 1975. *Foundations of language development.* London: UNESCO Press.

Leopold, W. F. 1939. *Speech development of a bilingual child: A linguist's record. Vol. I, Vocabulary growth in the first two years.* Evanston, Ill.: Northwestern University Press.

———. 1947. *Speech development of a bilingual child: A linguist's record. Vol. II, Sound learning in the first two years.* Evanston, Ill.: Northwestern University Press.

———. 1949a. *Speech development of a bilingual child: A linguist's record. Vol. III, Grammars and general problems in the first two years.* Evanston, Ill.: Northwestern University Press.

———. 1949b. *Speech development of a bilingual child: A linguist's record. Vol. IV, Diary from age two.* Evanston, Ill.: Northwestern University Press.

MacNamara, J. 1967. Bilingualism in the modern world. *Journal of Social Issues* 23: 1–7.

Menyuk, P. 1971. *The acquisition and development of language.* Englewood Cliffs, N.J.: Prentice-Hall, Inc.

Padilla, A. M., and Liebman, E. 1975. Language acquisition in the bilingual child. *The bilingual review/La revista bilingue* 2: 34–55.

Pavlovitch, M. 1920. *Le language entantin: Acquisition de serve et de francais par un enfant serve.* Paris: Champion.

Ronjat, J. 1913. *Le développement de langage observé chez un enfant bilingue.* Paris: Champion.

Saville, M. R., and Troike, R. C. 1971. *A Handbook of bilingual education.* Washington, D.C.: TESOL.

Slobin, D. I. 1971. Developmental psycholinguistics. In *A survey of linguistic science*, ed. W. O. Dingwall. College Park: University of Maryland Linguistics Program.

Smith, M. E. 1935. A study of the speech of eight bilingual children of the same family. *Child Development* 6: 19–25.

Snow, C. E. 1972. Mother's speech to children learning language. *Child Development* 43: 549–65.

Stockwell, R. P., Bowen, J. D., and Martin, J. W. 1965. *The grammatical structures of English and Spanish.* Chicago: University of Chicago Press.

Appendix 2.1

Rules for Calculating Mean Length
of Utterance for English

1. Start with the first utterance of the transcription.

2. Only fully transcribed utterances are used; none with blanks. Portions of utterances, entered in parentheses to indicate doubtful transcription, are used.

3. Include all exact utterance repetitions (marked with a plus sign in records). Stuttering is marked as repeated efforts at a single word; count the word once in the most complete form produced. In the few cases where a word is produced for emphasis or the like (no, no, no) count *each* utterance.

4. Do not count such fillers as "mm" or "oh," but do count "no," "yeah," and "hi."

5. All compound words (two or more free morphemes), proper names, and ritualized reduplications count as single words. Examples: birthday, rackety-boom, choo-choo, quack-quack, night-night, pocketbook, see saw. Justification is that no evidence that the constituent morphemes function as such for these children.

6. Count as one morpheme all irregular past of the verb (got, did, want, saw). Justification is that there is no evidence that the child relates these to present forms.

7. Count as one morpheme all diminutives (doggie, mommie) because these children at least do not seem to use the suffix

productively. Diminutives are the standard forms used by the child.

8. Count as separate morphemes all auxiliaries (is, have, will, can, must, would). Also all catenatives: gonna, wanna, hafta. These later counted as single morphemes rather than as "going to" or "want to" because evidence is that they function so for the children. Count as separate morphemes all inflections, for example, possessive(s), plural(s), third person singular(s), regular past(d), progressive(i).

Appendix 2.2

Rules for Calculating Mean Length of Utterance for Spanish

1. Start with first utterance.

2. Only fully transcribed utterances are uses; none with blanks. Portions of utterances, entered in parentheses to indicate doubtful transcription, are used.

3. Include all exact utterance repetitions (marked with a plus sign in records). Stuttering is marked as repeated efforts at a single word; count the word once in the most complete form produced. In the few cases where a word is produced for emphasis or the like (no, no, no) count each occurrence.

4. Do not count such fillers as "eh," "mm," or "oh," but do count "no," "sí," "oye," "ese," "hola."

5. All compound words (two or more free morphemes), proper names, and ritualized reduplications count as single words. Examples: *rompecabezas*/puzzle, *sacapuntas*/pencil sharpener, *cumpleaños*/birthday, *abrelatas*/can opener. Justification is that no evidence that the constituent morphemes function as such for these children.

6. Count as one morpheme all irregular pasts of the verb (hice, fui, poner). Justification is that there is no evidence that the child relates these to present forms.

7. Count as one morpheme all diminutives (perrito, mamá/

mamacita) because these children at least do not seem to use the suffix productively. Diminutives are standard forms used by the child.

8. Count as separate morphemes all auxiliaries. Examples: Dudo que él *puede* ir. ¿*Sabe* usted jugar al golf?—auxiliary "can." Ella *podía* cantar bien (auxiliary "could").
Pablo no *pudo* terminar el trabajo.
Usted *debería* ir a verlos (auxiliary "should").
Yo sabía que *debía* buscarle.

9. Count as separate morphemes all inflections, for example, plural(s, es) casa*s*, tren*es*; progressive (iendo, ando)—com*iendo*, tom*ando*.

10. Count as separate morphemes all single articles (el, la, etc.) and demonstrative pronouns (esta, este, etc.).

11. Count as separate morphemes all contractions (de, el— *del*, a, el—*al*). (Viene *del* norte. Vamos *al* cine.) These seem to be standard forms.

12. Count as additional morphemes article-noun and pronoun-noun agreement for both number and gender (el pato, los patos; *el* is scored as two morphemes because it agrees in number and gender with *pato*).

3

The Bilingual's
Linguistic-Social Environment

Incidence of Bilingualism

Regardless of the specific languages involved, it seems relatively safe to conclude that children are capable of learning more than one language during the years prior to formal education. The strongest evidence comes from two naturally occurring sources. The first is from societies throughout the world that "require" linguistic competence in more than one language. Sorenson (1967) describes the acquisition of three to four linguistically separate communicative forms by the young children of the northwest Amazon region of South America. Although Tukano tribal language serves as the *lingua franca* in this area, there continue to exist some twenty-five clearly distinguishable linguistic groups in this Brazilian-Colombian border region. In our own country, a multitude of linguistic groups considered bilingual by our previous definition continue to survive. The largest in the Spanish-speaking population are estimated (conservatively) at near 6.5 million in 1974. As Table 3.1 indicates, the majority of this population is located in five Southwestern states (Arizona, California, Colorado, New Mexico, and Texas) and can be ethnically classified as Mexican-American. Although this is the case, substantial numbers of this population are located

TABLE 3.1

Population of Spanish Origin by Selected Areas and Type of Origin

Area and Origin	Number
United States:	
Mexican-American	6,455,000
Puerto Rican	1,548,000
Cuban-American	689,000
Central or South American	705,000
aOther Spanish	1,398,000
TOTAL	10,795,000
Southwestern States:	
Mexican-American	5,453,000
Puerto Rican	62,000
Other Spanish	806,000
TOTAL	6,319,000

Source: Data presented here is constructed from the March 1974 Current Population Reports, U.S. Department of Commerce (1975a).

aThis category includes population of Spanish-speaking origin not included in the above categories.

throughout the United States. For instance, John and Horner (1971) suggest one-fourth of school-aged children in both New York and Chicago are of this linguistic population.

Spanish is only one language of several which are spoken by our native bilinguals. Other languages combining with English in early childhood for large segments of our population include Navaho (and other Native American languages), French, Russian, Chinese, Japanese, Portuguese, German, and Italian. Recent funding patterns by the Department of Education indicate the formal recognition of over seventy bilingual population groups in this country. This formal recognition is evidenced by funding of bilingual education programs for these groups as authorized by legislation aimed at funding bilingual schooling in the United States (Dissemination Center for Bilingual-Bicultural Education 1974).

A second form of evidence also clearly suggests the capacity of children to acquire more than one language during early child-hood. This source of evidence comes from parents visiting a foreign country for an extended period of the child's life. In these cases, the child is exposed to one language spoken in his home, while, external to this environment, another language is the most functional. Dato (1970) as reported by Cazden (1972) investigated the development of Spanish in his own four-year-old boy as well as four other children who were visiting Spain and who were encountering Spanish for the first time. More recently, Rosansky (1976) has provided a detailed description of a Spanish-speaking five-year-old child acquiring English during her parents' visit to the United States. Each of these studies, combined with the numerous anecdotal success stories by par-ents of their children's second language acquisition, corroborate the widespread existence of early childhood bilingualism.

Recent reported work on the maintenance of bilingualism sug-gests that the phenomenon is not one that will soon disappear. Spolsky (1970) in a survey of Navaho six-year-old children found that 73 percent of this population were "dominant" in their na-tive Navaho, although all children could be considered bilingual. This situation does not seem to be moving in the direction of English-only acquisition. Moreover, maintenance of both En-glish and Spanish systems among young preschool children of the southwestern United States has continued for the last one hundred years. Little evidence predicting the occurrence of di-minished bilingualism has been reported. A significant influence on the maintenance or increase of interest in early childhood bilingualism rests on the formal adoption of more than one lan-guage in certain countries (such as Canada) and informal adop-tion in other countries (English in European countries). The increasing closeness of our world neighbors, brought about by economic, political, and social necessities in combination with technological advances in travel and communication, suggests the continued emerging importance of bilingualism. It is there-fore clear that bilingualism (or multilingualism) is here to stay and will continue to rise.

Linguistic Input
The remainder of this chapter attempts to provide a relevant conceptual and empirical discussion of the linguistic and social

systems which affect early childhood bilingualism. In this manner, the discussion moves us beyond the general realization that bilingualism is an important and widespread phenomenon and into more specific and empirical aspects of bilingualism.

Linguistic Information   It seems appropriate to consider first in this discussion of specific conditions of bilingual acquisition the surrounding environment of the child, with an initial focus on the linguistic environment.

> If a complete record were available on the linguistic input presented to a subject during his life, it would be possible to generate a function describing the changes with age in the linguistic information presented. Linguistic information, in its simplest form, refers to the accumulative number of different word relations presented, whereas linguistic input denotes the total number of word relations regardless of whether they occurred only once or repeatedly (Riegel 1968, p. 648).

Any chronological record of this type coupled with a child's linguistic output would allow a very important correlational analysis of language development. Although this extensive information remains unavailable, some systematic semblance is becoming available for monolingual English children (Brown and Fraser 1963; Brown 1973; Schacter, Kirshner, Dilps, Friedricks, and Sanders 1974; Bowerman 1975; Braine 1976; Snow and Fergeson 1977). Unfortunately, little information of this caliber is available for young bilingual children.

Although this absence of empirical data is crippling, some cautious theoretical notions concerning bilingual input and its relationship to acquisitional success might prove useful. Some percentage of the child's linguistic information is in one language and some other meaningful percentage is in a second language. Mathematically, the extent of bilingualism might be considered as directly related to the proportion of language information made available in each language. In fact, language information made available to any speaker decreases with the age of that speaker such that close to one-half of the linguistic information available will be depleted during the first few years of life. (Information is defined here as the accumulated number of different word relations, not the total number of word relations regardless of difference.)

Using this assumption as a base, Riegel (1968) has generated a series of mathematical formulae which predict the degree of bilingualism as a function of the proportion of linguistic input in each language. These predictions, for the most part, consider the case of second language acquisition only. The bilingual situation where input in each language is near "simultaneous" in nature is more difficult to interpret using this theoretical model. Moreover, the model stresses as most important the quantity of linguistic information presented the learner for each language. In doing so, it disregards the psychological (cognitive development, information processing) and physiological (neural development) constraints discussed earlier in Chapter 1. There are also variations in the languages themselves. That is, the quantity of linguistic information may differ significantly between languages as a function of the individual linguistic structures available within each language. (The quality of the information presented to the learner may also differ as a function of the language system itself.) Additionally, in such a model, the languages to which the learner is exposed are considered totally independent. At present such an assumption seems empirically unwarranted. Therefore, a model which considers only the quantity of bilingual input in determining the extent of bilingualism falls short in considering the "gestalt" of bilingual acquisition. Yet any comprehensive model of bilingual acquisition must consider important the availability of linguistic information.

Compound-Coordinate Bilingualism   A more traditional theoretical treatment which has attempted to deal with interlingual relationships is best expressed by the concepts of compound and coordinate bilingualism (Weinreich 1953; Ervin and Osgood 1954; Lambert and Rawlings 1969). With respect to linguistic input, this distinction refers to the simultaneous or sequential exposure to two languages: compound bilinguals have acquired their languages in the same environmental surroundings within the same temporal and environmental contexts; coordinate bilinguals have acquired their languages in different temporal and environmental contexts. This distinction has typically been applied to adults who have equal competence in two languages but who have acquired their competence under these different circumstances.

The issue of central interest with the compound-coordinate

distinction has been the hypothesized form of linguistic processing generated by the linguistic contexts. Weinreich (1953) must be given partial credit for the initial proposed difference in linguistic processing as a function of the circumstances under which bilinguals acquired the specific symbols and rules of each language. With respect to lexical pairs, he characterized this relationship in three ways: coordinate pairs would have separate symbols (words) and separate meanings; compound pairs would have separate symbols but only one meaning; and subordinate pairs would have separate symbols and share some characteristics of similar meaning and some differences in meaning (this last category accounts for words which are learned through translation). Weinreich was careful to point out that any pair of symbols for any speaker may be either compound or coordinate and that any pair may move from coordinate to compound or vice versa as a function of that person's experience.

As Lopez (1977) reports, this trio of theoretically defined relationships was altered by Ervin and Osgood (1954). By concluding that both the compound and the subordinate pairs in both languages are associated with the same meaning, they subsumed the subordinate classification into the compound classification. Unfortunately, this logic brought together under one theoretical term (compound bilingualism) both those individuals who learned two languages simultaneously (usually as children) and those who learned a second language with assistance from the first (usually as adults). Most research in this area has directly or indirectly promoted each of these categories (for any one individual) as a total system. Jacobovitz and Lambert (1961), Kolers (1968), and Lambert and Rawlings (1969) have produced significant results indicating that compound bilinguals differed from coordinate bilinguals on linguistic tasks which called for the processing of mixed language associative networks (recall tasks which made use of translated equivalants). Other, more recent experiments have obtained similar results (Lopez and Young 1974; Lopez, Hicks, and Young 1974). These results might suggest that compound and coordinate bilinguals differ generally in language-processing attributes. This type of systems approach would not allow any one individual to vary within these two categories at any one point in time or to move from one category to another across time.

Unfortunately, the compound-coordinate phenomenon may be restricted to specific linguistic tasks. Kolers (1963) and Lambert (1969) both report no difference between compound and coordinate groups on some mixed-language tasks. Recently, reported research (Dillon et al. 1973; Newby 1976) which has tested mixed-language associative skills using short-term memory techniques also indicates results counter to the compound-coordinate theoretical distinction. These types of contradictions suggest that this theoretical conceptualization may be task related.

Owing to the above definitional problems in conjunction with reported empirical results, it still remains appropriate to conclude (MacNamara 1967, p. 60) that "the overall status of the distinction between coordinate and compound bilinguals, and consequently its theoretical importance, is difficult to assess." With respect to early childhood bilingual acquisition this distinction is even more confused. If one considers that children are processing phonological, morphological, syntactic, and semantic information in both languages and that information may differ across physical and social contexts, the compound-coordinate distinction seems to be psychologically meaningless. It is reasonable to suggest that any child operating within such a bilingual environment may be compound, coordinate, or some mixture of the two across contextual and linguistic parameters.

The Developmental Quality of Linguistic Input   The above discussion of linguistic input has been concerned with quantitative and temporal (simultaneous or separate) aspects of bilingual input. It has disregarded linguistic variation as it relates to this same information, that is, the particular quality of linguistic information in any one language. Although it seems clear that children are in no need of a qualitatively "rich" linguistic environment in order to achieve high levels of linguistic competence, the exact minimum input necessary for successful acquisition is very much still an empirical question. For the child learning more than one language, this same issue remains ambiguous.

Borrowing again from extensive research with monolingual children, it is appropriate to conclude that linguistic information varies qualitatively in several important areas. First, from a developmental perspective, linguistic information is identifiably different for younger children than older children. Snow and Fergeson (1977) summarize these characteristic changes as regularized linguistic expansions in the speech of parents, older siblings, and strangers to young children. That is, at early ages prior to any major developed linguistic repertoire, linguistic input directed at children is characterized by short, clear, highly pitched, and indexical forms (example, "Want cookie?"). This input is not characteristic of adult speech to children but of older siblings' or peer speech to children. This sort of directed input changes systematically to more elongated forms of interactional speech. Still other linguistic input characteristics are identifiable. Expansion (linguistic extensions of children's abbreviated utterances) and repetition (imitation) are two other such characteristics identified and extensively investigated (Brown and Bellugi 1964; Bloom 1973).

The exact function of these input characteristics is not altogether clear. They may very well serve as instructional devices for "teaching" or "stressing" important linguistic features to children acquiring their native language (Slobin 1975). At present it is possible to confirm confidently only such regularized patterns of input while speculating on their presumed function.

For bilingual children, few research accounts of this sort are available. Yet it seems likely that some of these same characteristic patterns will hold, and that they too may well influence either linguistic acquisition or some aspect of language use. One study (Harris and Hassemer 1972) reports the use of a modeling procedure to increase the linguistic complexity of both Spanish and English syntax in bilingual children. These researchers were concerned primarily with the influence of modeling on syntactic use and/or acquisition, but used both bilingual Spanish-English and monolingual English children as subjects in order to assess any differential effects of modeling conditions owing to multilinguistic repertoires. They defined complexity in terms of absolute sentence length. After an initial measure of topic sentence responses, subjects were exposed to adult models of expanded sentence length. For bilingual subjects, both Spanish and English expanded models were introduced. Results of a posttreatment measure indicated a significant increase in complex sentence production by both bilinguals and monolinguals in English. Furthermore, bilinguals did not differ significantly from monolinguals in the production of English syntax and all produced significantly more complex sentence constructions in Spanish. Therefore, the modeling procedure positively influenced syntactic productions equally in English for both groups in addition to influencing Spanish syntax for the bilingual group.

Bilingual Mother-Child Discourse:
An Empirical Study

The following investigation was an exploratory study that attempted to provide an analysis of a set of tape-recorded mother-child interactions, in Spanish and English, of participants who came from Spanish-English home environments. Of specific interest were the instructional characteristics of these interactions as they relate to the languages themselves. That is, what aspects of these interactions are similar to previous conceptual treatments of teacher-student interactions during formal "instructional time" (lessons) at microinteractional levels (Mehan et al. 1976). The following characterized the subjects and setting of the study:

1. All mothers and children were part of a preschool bilingual-bicultural effort which was voluntary in nature. Therefore, it was clear that mothers were very much interested in their children learning both languages.

2. All mothers served on a cooperative basis as instructors at the preschool. Their duties included both curriculum development and implementation in both Spanish and English. Therefore, although professional guidance was provided, all mothers served as teachers in the school.

3. All recordings were obtained at the preschool. Although these were done individually with each mother-child pair and only general instructions concerning the interactive nature of these sessions were given, it is very likely that the teaching format experienced at the preschool influenced the nature of the recorded mother-child interactions.

4. Previous detailed linguistic analysis of Spanish interactions combined with a parallel set of English mother-child interactions for these pairs indicated the dominance of English speech for each of the children. This is not to say that children did not "know" or use Spanish, but their recorded English was

much further advanced linguistically than their recorded Spanish.

In performing the discourse analysis, the Mehan interactional analysis model (now available for analyzing the sequential organization of speech acts within classroom lessons) was modified for use. This model concentrates on the sequential characteristics of teacher initiations, student responses, and teacher evaluations. In so doing, it attempts to provide a qualitative analysis of interaction style by taking into consideration the individual nature of teacher and student utterances as well as their combined qualitative nature.

Initial review of the selected transcripts, coupled with a general understanding of the Mehan interaction analysis system for coding, yielded some necessary modifications to accommodate the nature of these interactions and type of data available (working from transcripts only). While keeping Mehan's sequential nature of initiation, reply, and evaluation intact, we renamed them to accommodate the dyadic discourse—mother initiation, child replies, and mother replies. The subheadings for each of these three sections were also similarly modified (see Table 3.2 for the Mehan Modified Model). The major additions in this modified model were child repetitions and mother repetitions. This addition was necessary because initial review of the transcripts revealed many repetitions by both participants (especially in the Spanish transcripts).

The analysis of interactions by language context produced interesting differences. For each of the three sections of the interactional sequence (mother initiation, child replies, mother replies) the number of type of initiations were transformed into percentages (for example, number of coded mother product elicitations over the total number of statements coded as mother initiations). This was done for each section of the sequence and thus a comparison of Spanish interactions with the English interactions was made possible.

Mother Elicitations: Spanish Versus English (Table 3.3)   In the Spanish discourse, mothers employed slightly more product elicitations (51.6 percent) than during English discourse (32.3 percent). Product elicitations were defined as elicitation acts to which the respondent was to provide a factual response. Typical

TABLE 3.2

Definition of Interactional Characteristics for the Modified Mehan Model

---

I. Mother Initiation
  A. Elicitations
    1. Choice
      An elicitation act in which the initiator provides responses in the elecitation itself. ("Is it blue or green?")
    2. Product
      An elicitation act to which the respondent is to provide a factual response. ("What is this?")
    3. Process
      An elicitation act which asks the respondent for opinions and interpretations. ("What is he doing?")
    4. Metaprocess
      An elicitation act which asks the respondent to be reflective on the process of reasoning itself. ("Why does he?")
  B. Directives
    These are preparatory exchanges designed to have respondents take specific actions. ("Look here.")
  C. Informatives
    An act which passes on information, facts, opinions, or ideas. ("This girl's dress is blue.")

II. Child Reply
  A. No reply
    Child does not answer initiation acts; silence for a 2-second period.
  B. Topic Relevant Reply
    1. Choice
      Choice response relevant to the initiator's topic ("blue").
    2. Product
      Product response relevant to initiator's topic ("car").
    3. Process
      Process response relevant to the initiator's topic. ("Playing with a dog.")
    4. Metaprocess
      Metaprocess response relevant to the initiator's topic. ("'Cause he's not scared.")

These responses were also scored: (1) if irrelevant to initiator's topic and (2) if relevant to initiator's previous topic.

C. Bid
These constitute statements which attempt to gain attention, i.e., change the topic. These can be considered as initiation by the child. ("What is this?")

D. Reaction
Negative acts taken in response to a directive. ("I don't want to.")

E. Repetition
Child repeats the previous mother statement either partially, exactly, or expanded.

F. Don't Understand
Child indicates he did not understand initiator. ("What?")

G. Irrelevant Reply
Uncodeable child reply.

III. Mother Reply

A. Repetition
Mother repeats previous child utterance either partially, exactly, or expanded.

B. Evaluation
Mother accepts (positive) or rejects (negative) previous child utterance. ("Okay, that's good"; "Not that way.")

C. Prompts
Statements given in response to incorrect, incomplete, or misunderstood replies. ("There are three.")

D. Child-Topic Initiator
Initiating statements in response to initiations by the child. (These were earlier designated as Child Bids: "There are two tigers.")

---

examples: in English, "What's this?"; in Spanish "¿Cómo se llama esto?" (Translated "What's this called?"). The higher percentage of product elicitations in the Spanish interaction and the nature of the product elicitations suggest the teaching of Spanish pronunciation and/or translation. For example:

Mother: "¿Qué es eso?"   ("What is that?")
Child: "Casa."   ("House.")
Mother: "Una casa, muy bien."   ("A house, very good.")

In this example, the mother asks a product-type question and receives a product response ("casa"). In Spanish discourse it

TABLE 3.3

Mother Elicitations

	Spanish	English
% Product	51.6	32.3
% Choice	1.6	19.7
% Process	6.9	19.3
% Informatives	26.3	22.5
% Directives	13.6	6.2
% Mother-determined	92.9	81.3
% Child-determined	7.1	18.7

was typical for the mother to request identification of an item in Spanish. Additionally, the mother was likely to restate the child's product response (and sometimes expand on it), possibly indicating that correct pronunciation was being modeled.

During English discourse, product elicitations may be typified as similar to those observed during Spanish discourse, except that in Spanish, pronunciation (or translation) was emphasized. That is, few child product responses were restated. In the Spanish context, the child seemed to be cued to pronunciation by stressed terms in the mother's elicitations. (This did not occur in the English interactions.) An example of this follows:

Mother: "Hay DOS ESCALERAS."   ("There are TWO LADDERS.")
Child: "Dos escaleras."   ("Two ladders.")

Choice elicitation percentages revealed major differences. Very few of these were elicited during Spanish discourse (1.6 percent) as compared to English discourse (19.7 percent). Process elicitations are defined as acts which ask the respondent for opinions and interpretations (e.g., "What's he doing?"). In English context, 19.3 percent of the total mother elicitations were of this process type while only 6.9 percent occurred in the Spanish context. This interesting finding along with the finding for choice elicitations seems to suggest strongly that the mother was modifying the discourse strategy by taking into consideration her

TABLE 3.4

Child Reply

	Spanish	English
% Product	22.4	27.1
% Choice	0	18.3
% Process	9.1	28.5
% Repetition	42.3	4.1
% No Reply	16.7	4.1
% Don't Understand	.7	1.6
% Irrelevant Reply	.2	.6
% Bid	8.6	15.7
% Successful	4.0	12.7
% Unsuccessful	4.6	3.0

child's linguistic capabilities. Mothers were emitting less process elicitations in Spanish than in English.

Child Replies: Spanish Versus English (Table 3.4)   Major differences occurred in three areas—choice response, process response, and repetitions. There were no choice responses in the Spanish interactions, while in the English 18.3 percent were coded. This could be expected given that in the Spanish context the mother asked very few choice questions (1.6 percent). The few process responses in the Spanish interactions (9.1 percent) as compared to the English (28.5 percent) can also be accounted for by the few process elicitations by the mother. The majority of child replies in the Spanish context were in the form of repetitions (42.3 percent), while in the English only 4.1 percent occurred. In the Spanish interactions, repetitions seemed to emphasize pronunciation. Mothers often stated a word with stress, the child repeated, then mother repeated, and so on. For example:

Mother: "Sonrisa."   ("Smile.")
Child: "Sonrisa."
Mother: "Sonrisa."
Child: "Sonrisa."

TABLE 3.5

Mother Reply

	Spanish	English
% Repetition	39.3	24.2
% Evaluation	33.9	27.9
% Positive	18.3	22.6
% Negative	15.6	5.3
% Prompt	26.8	47.9

Child bids (or child initiations), while similar in occurrence in both languages, were also coded as successful or unsuccessful in gaining attention or initiating a new topic. In the English interactions, the great majority (81.5 percent) were successful child initiations while slightly more than half of the Spanish context bids were unsuccessful.

Mother Replies: Spanish Versus English (Table 3.5)   The majority of all mother replies in the Spanish interactions were in the form of repetitions (39.3 percent). Again, this seems to reflect the mother's reinforcement of the child's Spanish pronunciation. While evaluations were relatively similar in occurrence, the type of evaluation (positive or negative) differed in both contexts. The Spanish context's positive and negative evaluations were somewhat evenly distributed, while in English positive evaluations were relatively more frequent.

Prompting was defined as statements in response to incorrect, incomplete, or misunderstood replies (e.g., "There are THREE!"). The majority of all mother replies in the English context were prompts (47.9 percent). The nature of these interactions (English) was such that the mother and child were continually building on each other's statements, the mother usually completing or adding where the child left off. The Spanish interaction prompts were related to incorrect pronunciation or request for the child to reply in Spanish (not English).

Discourse Analysis   Using the quantitative measures and qualitative structure of the mother-child interactions, different interactional models for each language interaction were determined. Initially, a general interactional model for both Spanish and English discourse can be generated:

General Discourse Model

```
mother elicitation ←┐        1st order
  ┌→child reply ──→   │        2nd order
  └─mother reply──→   │        3rd order
```

Using the above model, the interactional length of each topic, sequence was identified as first order, second order, third order, or fourth (or more) order interactions (see Table 3.6). First-order length is defined as a mother-initiated topic with the child either ignoring the topic by not replying, changing the topic by bidding, or the mother changing the topic after failing to elicit a response from the child. For example:

(1) Mother: "¿En dónde estan los niños?" ("Where are the children?")
    Child: No reply
    (Change topic)
(1) Mother: "¿Qué trae puesto la niña? ¿Qué es eso?"
               ("What is the girl wearing? What is that?")

While interactions coded as first order are not "true" interactions, they are attempts to start them. Second-order-length interactions can be typified by mother initiation of topic, the child replying, but with no mother reply:

(1) Mother: "¿Cómo se llama todo esto? Esta es una foto, un
               retrato de mucha gente."
               ("What is all this called? This is a picture, a picture
               of many people.")
(2) Child: "Azul"   ("Blue")
                    End of Topic

(1) Mother: "El está jugando con las pelotas."
               ("He is playing with the balls.")
(2) Child: "Pelotas"   ("Balls")
                    End of Topic

TABLE 3.6

Interaction Length

	Spanish	English
% 1st Order	11.6	14.9
% 2nd Order	36.3	53.8
% 3rd Order	36.1	12.7
% 4th Order	16.0	18.6

General Discourse Model

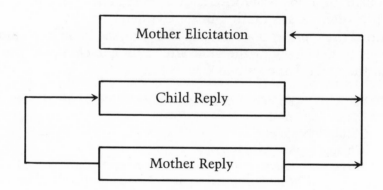

| (1) Mother: | "¿Eso qué es?" | ("What is that?") |
| (2) Child: | "Boca" | ("Mouth") |

End of Topic

Third-order interactions included three-part sequences:

(1) Mother:	"¿De qué color son los elefantes?"	
	("What color are the elephants?")	
(2) Child:	"Verde"	("Green")
(3) Mother:	"Verdes"	("Green")

End of Topic

Fourth-order-length interactions were made up of four-part sequences:

(1) Mother:	"¿Qué es?"	("What is it?")
(2) Child:	"Una silla"	("A chair")
(3) Mother:	"Silla del dentista"	("A dentist's chair")
(4) Child:	"Yeah"	

For more than fourth-order interactions, (3) and (4) above were repeated.

We tabulated the interaction lengths for each language interaction and found that a high percentage of the English interactions were of the second-order form (53.9 percent). This is primarily due to the nature of the interaction. The mother elicits a topic, the child replies, and the mother moves to a new topic. The major difference in language interactions was in the third-order form. The Spanish interaction used more third-order interaction sequences. This is possibly accounted for by high incidences of the mother's repeating the child's reply (as found in the high percentage of mother repetition replies—39.3 percent).

Spanish Discourse Model (Table 3.7)   In this model, the mother elicits a topic, the child repeats, then the mother replies. This sequence is followed by a new mother elicitation (new topic). Therefore, it is categorized primarily as a third-order form, or the mother elicits, child replies, then mother elicits a new topic (second-order form). The broken line in the illustration of the Spanish Interaction Model of Table 3.7 means that sometimes (but not often) the child builds onto the mother's reply usually with a new topic (child initiation).

English Discourse Model (Table 3.7)   This model differs from the Spanish in that the child tends to build on the mother's reply quite often (and usually with a new topic). The mother elicits, child replies, mother replies, child replies, then mother replies in a cyclical pattern (fourth or more order form), or the mother elicits, child replies, mother replies, then child replies followed by a mother elicitation (fourth-order form). But as the interaction-length data (Table 3.7) shows, the majority of the topics in this model are usually of the second-order form. That is, the mother elicits a topic, the child responds, and a new mother elicitation follows. This second-order form is similar to the Spanish interaction but differs qualitatively (see next sec-

TABLE 3.7

Spanish and English Discourse Models

Spanish Discourse Model

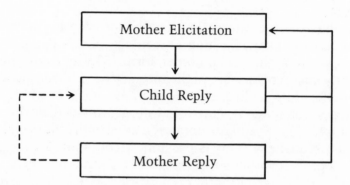

English Discourse Model

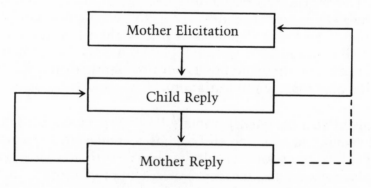

tion). The broken line in this model refers to the least-used path of mother elicitation: child reply, mother reply, followed by a new mother elicitation. At this point the Spanish and English discourse models differ. This difference seems to indicate that instruction is taking place in the Spanish interaction and not in the English. The Spanish interaction pattern seems to follow closely the classic Mehan sequence of instruction: teacher initiation—student reply—teacher evaluation. Spanish-English bilingual parents of this country wanted their preschool children to speak Spanish. He found that few of the parents, however, had an explicit strategy for implementing bilingualism. Parents relied only on the child's exposure to two languages in the home, and maintained that this was sufficient for their children to become proficient speakers of Spanish and English.

What seems to have surfaced in this study is that there may be an explicit strategy parents used in teaching their children two languages. However, this strategy may have surfaced because the mother was in a school setting, was considered a teacher, and believed in the aims of the bilingual-bicultural program which she helped to develop and implement. That is to say, the status of the school context may have contributed to the explicitness of teaching strategies which may not be present in home environments. Even with such constraints the present analysis provides new and interesting information. It signals as important the investigation of discourse strategies adopted by parents of bilingual children. The present analysis must be considered exploratory. Further studies of this nature should reveal the functional role of qualitative aspects of bilingual discourse and their relationship to early childhood bilingual acquisition.

Sociolinguistic Considerations

The recent interdisciplinary effort bringing together sociology, anthropology, and linguistics, which has been concerned with the linguistic environment of the bilingual, is the field of sociolinguistics (Hymes 1967). The focus of investigation within this field is purposefully broadly defined but can best be characterized as centering on the realization that language is embedded within some social contexts which cannot be ignored if we are to understand totally the function of linguistic behavior.

Fishman (1971) has been most critical of research in bilingualism which does not consider "domains of social interaction." These criticisms follow from extensive sociolinguistic research on Puerto Rican bilinguals in New York City during the late 1960s. These extensive observational, attitudinal, and experimental investigations clearly indicate the restrictedness of linguistic input and use in the various social domains examined. One such study will be described in detail here and should serve as an example of sociolinguistic concern for contextual influences of bilingualism at the input level. (Later discussions of bilingual functioning will consider yet another sociolinguistic concern: language mixing or code switching.)

Edelman (1969) reports an experiment which was a component of the overall research project undertaken by Fishman and his colleagues. In this particular study, young school-age Puerto Rican bilinguals were interviewed using a series of preformulated questions designed to assess the degree to which children used Spanish and English within social domains representative of education (school), religion (church), family (home), and neighborhood (playgrounds). In addition, students were presented with a word-naming task in which they were asked to name, within forty-five-second periods, as many objects as could be found in each of four settings: kitchen, school, church, and neighborhood. Children were asked to name these objects first in one language, then the other.

Results of this study mirror those found in several studies concerned with social contexts and bilingualism. Specifically, children reported using one language over another as a function of different social domains. These children reported using more Spanish in domains central to the family and neighborhood while using more English in the domains of education and religion. Older children produced more labels in general and more labels were produced in English than Spanish. Yet, in several domains specificity was again apparent. Using a dominance ratio derived from the relative number of labels produced in each language for each domain, the social domain of family was characterized by the smallest difference between Spanish and English, while education was characterized by the largest difference.

Contextual and Input Parameters: An Empirical Study

Findings like these suggest that the social context of language is a variable too powerful to be ignored. This seems especially true in our understanding of early childhood bilingualism resulting from the correlation of language function and social domain. The following account attempts to deal with this contextualization phenomenon at the preschool level. It is concerned with monitoring both English and Spanish use in two preschool environments.

The basic issue of interest was related to the sociolinguistic description of Spanish-English use by children and adults (the children's mothers) in two different preschool contexts: instruction periods, and freeplay periods. Additionally, an experimental attempt to influence the use of Spanish by children through the implementation of a Spanish "immersion" program (Lambert and Tucker 1972) during freeplay sessions was tested. The issue of language manipulation came out of the sociolinguistic description of language use in each setting. This description pointed out very consistently that children, in particular, were "choosing" since all children came from bilingual home environments and indicated some use of Spanish during instruction sessions.

Eight mothers and ten children (ranging from two years, ten months to two years, eleven months of age at the beginning of the study) who were involved in a coop bilingual preschool program served as subjects. The classes were held in a twelve-by-fourteen-foot instruction area and a twelve-by-twelve-foot freeplay area. The room designated as the instruction room was equipped with two large tables, chairs, and a movable blackboard. The freeplay area contained miscellaneous tables, toys, and play equipment. The use of the Spanish and/or English languages by the primary participants involved in the preschool settings was the dependent measure of interest. The occurrence of Spanish and/or English was recorded by an observer for both children and mothers within ten-second intervals. The use of Spanish and/or English included a minimum of one word. Such words as the children's or mothers' names (that is, Juan, Joe, Mary, Dolores, etc.) and the use of the words *no* and *mama* were excluded. There were only two limitations for not recording language use. If the mother left the primary room and the students were alone, recordings were not made of any language outside the room by the mother (i.e., teachers step out to the hall). If the children left the room of primary use, no recordings were made of the children outside the room (i.e., child goes to restroom).

Observations were taken for twenty minutes on each set of

mothers during freeplay periods. The instructional period was the time when specific curriculum tasks were presented by mothers; during freeplay no specific instruction took place. Throughout the study, mothers were told in both Spanish and English when observers were recording how much English and Spanish was used. Reliability (interobserver agreement) was computed by session for each category of response. Session reliability during the twenty-six weeks of the study ranged between 69 and 100 percent (with a mean of 89.36 percent and a median of 93 percent) across the four categories of responses recorded.

During the first nineteen weeks of the study, there was never any attempt to increase or decrease Spanish or English in either preschool activity. Owing to the very low measure of Spanish for children during freeplay sessions, an attempt to increase Spanish was implemented with the additional concern that any change should be experimentally replicated. In order to accomplish these two goals a series of experimental manipulations were introduced. First, two weeks (eight sessions) were designated as Baseline. These sessions were similar to previous ones in that no attempt was made to influence language introduction.

After the completion of this two-week period, mothers were given the following instructions prior to each freeplay session:

Cuando entren al cuarto de juegos, por favor hablan no más en inglés. Si los niños les hablan en inglés, pídenles hablar en español, y no les respondan en inglés. [This statement asks the mother to speak only in Spanish, to ask the children to speak in Spanish if they speak to them (the mothers) in English, but to speak always in Spanish.]

Small written signs ("Hablan en Español") were also placed on the walls of the freeplay area during this part of the study. This part will be referred to as Immersion I and was implemented for three consecutive weeks (twelve sessions).

After completion of the above conditions, a return to Baseline procedures was established. Observational procedures continued, but mothers were not given any special instructions prior to freeplay sessions. (Signs were removed from the freeplay area.) After a two-week period, immersion procedures were again implemented during freeplay sessions (Immersion 2). These manipulations allowed an experimental evaluation of immersion effects making use of a within group ABAB experimental design (Baer, Wolf, and Risley 1968).

Figure 1 presents the mean percentage of intervals in which Spanish was recorded for mothers and children in each of the two preschool settings for successive weeks of the study. During instruction settings, Spanish was higher for mothers than for children (a total mean of 56 percent for mothers and 15 percent for children). This seemed to remain somewhat stable over the nineteen weeks of the study. In freeplay sessions, mothers' use of Spanish was more variable (with a mean of 34 percent), while children's usage was consistently near zero (a mean of 4 percent). In general then, mothers' Spanish was much higher than children's, and both mothers and children showed evidence of increased and more stable use of Spanish during instruction sessions than during freeplay sessions.

Figure 2 presents the mean percentage of intervals in which English was recorded for mothers and children in each of the two preschool settings for successive weeks of the study. During instruction, English usage was near 50 percent for both mothers and children (a total of 51 percent for mothers and 44 percent for children). However, during freeplay, children's English was consistently higher than mothers' (a total mean of 75 percent for children and 43 percent for mothers). Mothers' English measures were more variable (ranging between 16 and 77 percent) than were the children's (range was from 56 to 82 percent).

Figure 3 presents the percentage of intervals in which Spanish was recorded for both mothers and children in each setting of the preschool for successive sessions of the experimental study. Figure 4 presents similar information for English measures. Table 4 presents the mean percentage of intervals Spanish and English use was observed in instruction and freeplay sessions for mothers and children during the four experimental conditions. During freeplay sessions of the Baseline section, Spanish usage remained constant for children (mean of 5 percent) and for mothers (mean of 39 percent). Therefore, Spanish measures during instruction sessions and English measures during both instruction and freeplay sessions continued at the same general levels observed during the first nineteen-week observation period. During Immersion 1, an increase occurred in Spanish for

Figure 3.1. Mean percentage of intervals in which Spanish was recorded for mothers and children in each preschool setting for successive weeks of the study.

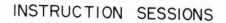

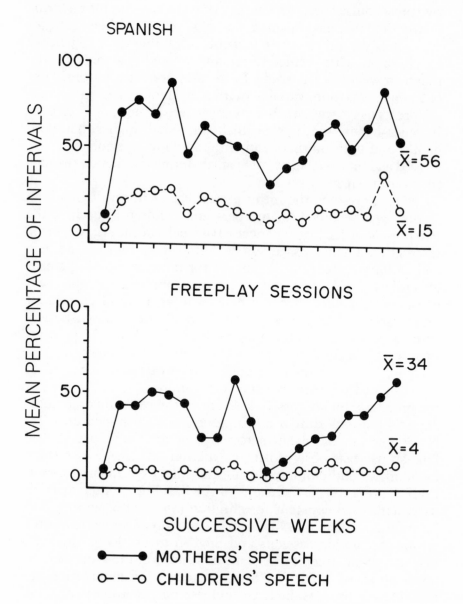

Figure 3.2. Mean percentage of intervals in which English was recorded for mothers and children in each preschool setting for successive weeks of the study.

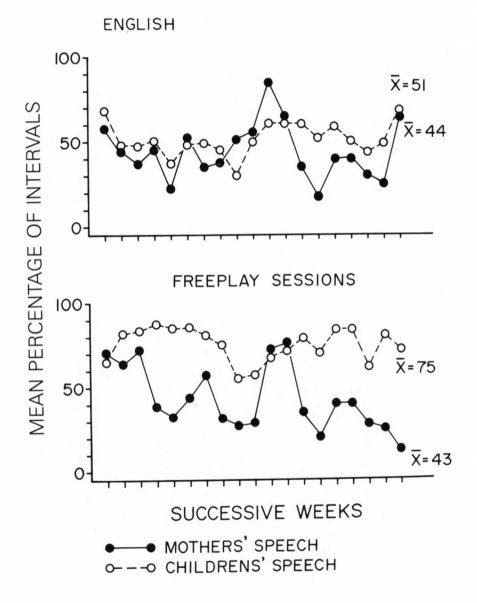

INSTRUCTION SESSIONS

ENGLISH

Figure 3.3. Percentage of intervals in which Spanish was recorded for mothers and children in each preschool setting for successive sessions of experimental study. Dotted vertical lines indicate changes in experimental manipulations in another setting. Solid vertical lines indicate changes in experimental manipulations within that setting.

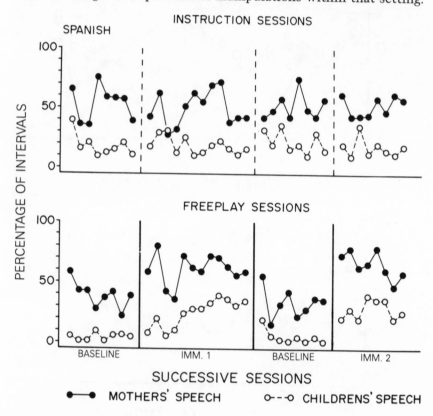

Figure 3.4. Percentage of intervals in which English was recorded for mothers and children in each preschool setting for successive sessions of the experimental study. Dotted vertical lines indicate changes in experimental conditions in another setting and/or with another language.

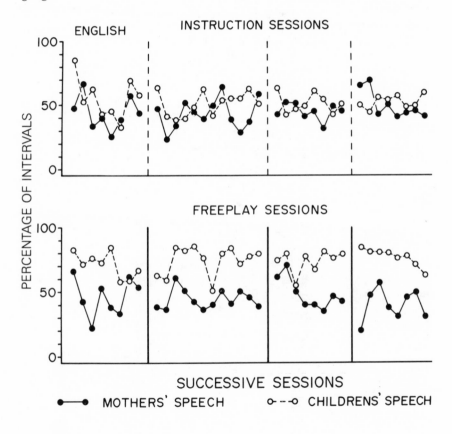

SUCCESSIVE SESSIONS

●——● MOTHERS' SPEECH   ○--○ CHILDRENS' SPEECH

TABLE 3.8

Mean Percentage of Intervals Spanish and English[1]

Experimental Conditions	English				Spanish			
	Instruction		Freeplay		Instruction		Freeplay[a]	
	Mother	Child	Mother	Child	Mother	Child	Mother	Child
Baseline	44	55	46	71	54	18	39	5
Immersion #1	44	51	44	71	50	18	61	23
Baseline	45	51	49	73	51	22	33	4
Immersion #2	50	53	43	77	53	18	63	28

[a]Only sessions in which experimental manipulation occurred.
1. Mean percentage of intervals Spanish and English was observed in instruction and freeplay sessions for mothers and children by successive conditions of the experiment.

both mothers and children during freeplay sessions. For mothers the increase was immediate, then stabilized. The increase in mean performance was from 39 percent in Baseline to 61 percent during Immersion 1. Children's measures of Spanish increased gradually then stabilized. The increase in mean performance was from 5 to 23 percent. There were no other changes evident from Baseline to Immersion 1 for Spanish measures during instruction sessions or English measures during instruction and freeplay sessions.

The return to Baseline resulted in a decrease in Spanish measures in freeplay sessions for both mothers and children (means of 33 percent and 4 percent, respectively). Mothers' measures tended to be variable while children's measures remained near zero. No other clear changes in performance were apparent for other Spanish or English measures. An immediate increase in Spanish for both mothers and children occurred with the reintroduction of the immersion procedures. (Means for this condition were 63 percent for mothers and 28 percent for children.) Once performance increased, it seemed to stabilize for each group. Again, no other changes in performance occurred for other measures of Spanish or English. (See Table 3.8.)

The present study attempted to combine sociolinguistic methodology with that of experimental manipulation. Of interest were the language-use patterns of bilingual mothers and children participating in a bilingual preschool program. Systematic observations of Spanish and English were undertaken on a daily basis over a nineteen-week period in two settings of the preschool (instruction and freeplay sessions). Also, an experimental manipulation in the form of a Spanish immersion program was implemented during selected freeplay sessions. This manipulation was performed in order to test the influence of immersion techniques (reported by Lambert and Tucker 1972) within this specific preschool format.

Prior to any detailed discussion of these data, it is important to point out that the mothers and children who participated in this study came from bilingual home environments (although the degree of bilinguality may have differed among participants). In addition, the preschool which they attended considered the development of bilinguality as its most important function. The concept and practice of bilingual education was relatively new to these families' environments. Also, the bilingual population in the area was very small (estimated at less than 10 percent). Therefore, any conclusion from these data must keep in mind the social circumstances of the participants both within the confines of the preschool and those of their own community.

Results from the nineteen-week observational study can be summarized as follows: More Spanish was observed for mothers during instruction sessions than freeplay sessions, although Spanish was used substantially in both settings. More Spanish was observed for mothers during each setting as compared to that observed for children (almost three or four times more Spanish was recorded for mothers); children used little during instruction sessions (mean of 15 percent) and almost none during freeplay sessions (mean of 4 percent). English was used by mothers in almost equal amounts during instruction and freeplay settings. More English was observed for children in freeplay than in instruction sessions. More English was used than Spanish by children in each setting.

In general, while mothers used both languages frequently in each preschool setting, children used primarily English, especially during freeplay sessions.

Although it is impossible from these data to determine the causal agents operating within these different contexts, some cautious observations may be of value. First, the present bilingual education effort had little influence on the observed use of Spanish and English among the children of the study during freeplay periods. They were producing little Spanish while at the same time producing large quantities of English. It is important to point out that the criterion reference test given to these children indicated that the children were acquiring the curriculum material in both languages—they were bilingual.

Results of the experimental procedure seem clear. During implementation of the immersion procedure in freeplay sessions, mothers' and children's use of Spanish increased substantially, and, increases did not occur until this technique was implemented. Since no qualitative data are available, it is difficult to assess the nature of those or linguistic variables responsible for these changes. It is likely that mothers used explicit instructions to the children; by using more Spanish, mothers set the occasion for more use of Spanish by children; mothers ignored

English and attended only to Spanish; or some combinations of all of the above three alternatives. Regardless of the exact causal variables, the outcome of the present experimental manipulations suggests a possible global variable which may serve to increase selected language use.

In summary, then, the present study has reaffirmed the importance of sociolinguistic information within educational environments. It has suggested specifically that bilingual education programs must be concerned with the child's total environment if bilinguality is to be a general educational goal. Furthermore, it has suggested (and preliminarily tested) one specific technique for increasing selected language. Of course, more exhaustive work is needed in this area to identify the specific causal agents involved in this demonstration.

Other Social (Cultural) Considerations

If we concede that social variables are indeed important to consider within the present context of bilingualism, and that treating linguistic entities independent of social networks is inadequate, the concept of culture as a heuristic seems reasonable. It is difficult to decide whether cultures influence individuals or individual events create culture. I will remain "on the fence" with respect to this issue, assuming that influences occur in both directions. The notion I wish to stress here is that of biculturalism. This term is used widely to describe the cultural attributes which characterize individuals who are raised in a situation in which recognized cultures are in contact. This concept not only implies that an individual in such a situation exemplifies attributes of two cultures, but that the two separate "parent" cultures in contact produce unique, hybrid attributes (forms of behavior) not common to either of the two parent cultures.

Just as with our earlier discussion of linguistic characteristics, cultural characteristics cannot be seen as either homogeneous or stable. There is no such thing as a "middle-class" culture. Instead, there are variations of something we can empirically identify as "middle class," just as there is a language we can empirically define as "standard" English. What does seem clear is that individuals who come from diverse linguistic environments also come from relatively diverse cultural environments. Their norms of social interaction, for instance, are subject to influence by this intermixing of cultures which surrounds them. All children in any culture at early stages of development are the product of specific influences of their interactions with their immediate environment (family, peers, other aspects of the small external world). In later years other external influences, including educational influences, broaden the scope of cultural impact. But, what of the early years? Is biculturalism or multiculturalism a valid and useful conceptualization during early childhood?

The relationship between bilingualism and biculturalism in early childhood is one which is not clearly understood. The most often cited relationship of these two variables has centered around the hypothetical construct of "self-concept." Studies of "self-concept" of Mexican-American children in this country suggest that the rejection of a child's home language (a component of his culture) when in contact with diverse social settings leads to psychological maladjustment. Ramírez (1977) and Castañeda (1977) suggest that this rejection of a child's language leads to low self-esteem which in turn results in poor achievement (usually measured by educationally related variables). Some evidence of this relationship is presented by Ramírez and Castañeda (1974). After extensive analysis of bilingual children who were participating in a bilingual/bicultural education program, these authors conclude that these students

> scored significantly higher on a measure of self esteem at the end of the year than at the beginning of the year. The children showed signs of better adjustment to school and were less frequently absent from school than children from comparable control classrooms (Ramírez and Castañeda 1974, p. 63).

Unfortunately, the relationship between self-concept and linguistic acquisition in either one or two languages has not been directly addressed. Therefore, it remains difficult to draw any generalizations from school achievement studies in this area. A major problem is the difficulty of obtaining reliable and valid measures of self-concept in young children. Therefore, discussion of it here reflects more the general research on bilingualism and not its necessary importance to early childhood bilingualism. Given this dilemma, it is not likely that self-concept, as used in our earlier discussions, has bearing as a useful conceptual tool in understanding early childhood bilingualism. This, of course, may prove to be false in the near future. As Price-Williams (1976) suggests, the study of cultural differences as it relates to psychological processes is in its infant stages. It awaits new theoretical, methodological, and technical advancement.

Still the notion of bilingualism and its influence on the acquisition of more than one language can be useful. This conclusion is based on our previous discussion of the sociolinguistic corollary which suggests that language must not only be learned, but the social rules governing the use of language must also be acquired. It is very likely that social situations which can be identified as culturally different, based on valid norms of cultural attributes, may convey different rules for language use.

This observation has led to a systematic analysis of communicative differences under the heading of the Ethnography of Speaking (Hymes 1967; Bauman and Sherzer 1975). This view considers language as a functional entity. A speech act is viewed from a functional perspective as a way of doing something with verbal signals:

> It is in this sense that a community's range of speech acts constitute means for the conduct of speaking—they represent conventionalized ways of doing things with words, ready-organized building blocks with which to construct discourse (Bauman and Sherzer 1975, pp. 106–7).

It is these considerations which lead to a social-interaction definition of language or speech which focuses on the frequency of social interaction and communication patterns within or between groups of a given speech community. With respect to frequency of interaction, Phillips (1972) contrasted Native American speech activities on the Warm Springs Indian reservation with non-Native American speech in school classrooms, with respect to the functional use of interspersed silence and speech activities. Labov (1970) has focused on communicative patterns of black English-speakers with an investigatory emphasis on the linguistic features of phonology and grammar. These studies relate linguistic features in various linguistic contexts to social groupings (same or different social group listeners) and situational contexts (physically identifiable characteristics of speech settings). Bauman and Sherzer (1975) have reported that the Chamula metaphor for heat, which operates in a multitude of utterances, is always ritualistic in nature.

It is these social-contextual situations which face the young children operating in linguistically diverse environments whose difference is characterized by more than linguistic features. Linguistic differences are socially salient, and the language within each helps determine this saliency. It is important then to recognize the complex nature of early childhood bilinguals with respect to the social systems in which languages are embedded and which they in turn assist in determining. The unfortunate lack of research with respect to these variables must be corrected, with a clearer understanding of bilingualism and biculturalism the ultimate goal.

References

Baer, D. M., Wolf, M. M., and Risley, T. R. 1968. Some current dimensions of applied behavior analysis. *Journal of Applied Behavior Analysis* 1: 91–97.

Bauman, R., and Sherzer, J. 1975. The ethnography of speaking. *Annual Review of Anthropology* 4: 95–117.

Bloom, L. 1973. *One word at a time: The use of single word utterances before syntax.* The Hague: Mouton.

Bowerman, M. 1975. Crosslinguistic similarities at two stages of syntactic development. In *Foundations of language development,* eds. E. Lenneberg and E. Lenneberg, vol. I, pp. 267–82. London: UNESCO Press.

Braine, M. D. S. 1976. *Children's first word combinations.* Monographs of the Society for Research in Child Development.

Brown, R. 1973. *A first language: The early stages.* Cambridge, Mass.: Harvard University Press.

Brown, R., and Bellugi, U. 1964. Three processes in the child's acquisition of syntax. *Harvard Educational Review* 34: 133–51.

Brown, R., and Fraser, D. 1963. The acquisition of syntax. In *Verbal Behavior and Learning,* eds. C. N. Cofer and B. Musgrave, pp. 113–46. New York: McGraw-Hill.

Castañeda, A. 1977. Traditionalism, modernism, and ethnicity. In *Chi-*

cano psychology, ed. J. Martinez, pp. 355–60. New York: Academic Press.

Cazden, C. B. 1972. *Child language and education*. New York: Holt, Rinehart & Winston.

Dillon, R. F., McCormack, P. D., Petrusie, W. M., Cook, G. M., and LaFleur, L. 1973. Release from proactive interference in compound and coordinate bilinguals. *Bulletin of the Psychomic Science* 2: 293–94.

Dissemination Center for Bilingual Bicultural Education. 1974. *Guide to Title VII*. Austin, Texas: ESEA Bilingual Bicultural Projects.

Edelman, M. 1969. The contextualization of school children's bilingualism. *Modern Language Journal* 53: 179–82.

Ervin, S. M., and Osgood, C. E. 1954. Second-language learning and bilingualism. *Journal of Abnormal and Social Psychology* 49: 139–46.

Fishman, J. 1971. *Bilingualism in the Barrio*. New York: Yeshiva University Press.

Gossen, G. H. 1974. To speak with a heated heart: Chamula canons of style and good performance. In *Exploration in the ethnography of speaking*, eds. R. Bauman and J. Sherzer, pp. 389–413. London: Cambridge University Press.

Harris, M. B., and Hassemer, W. G. 1972. Some factors affecting the complexity of children's sentences: The effect of modeling, age, sex, and bilingualism. *Journal of Experimental Child Psychology* 13: 447–55.

Hymes, D. 1967. Models of the interaction of language and social setting. *Journal of Social Issues* 23: 8–28.

Jacobovitz, L. A., and Lambert, W. E. 1961. Semantic satiation among bilinguals. *Journal of Experimental Psychology* 62: 516–82.

John, V. P., and Horner, V. M. 1971. *Early childhood bilingual education*. New York: Modern Language Association of America.

Kolers, P. A. 1963. Interlingual word associations. *Journal of Verbal Learning and Verbal Behavior* 2: 291–300.

Kuo, E. C. 1974. The family and bilingual socialization: A sociolinguistic study of a sample of Chinese children in the United States. *Journal of Social Psychology* 92: 181–91.

Labov, W. 1970. *The study of nonstandard English*. Urbana, Ill.: National Council of Teachers of English.

Lambert, W. E. 1969. Psychological studies of the interdependencies of the bilingual's two languages. In *Substance and structure of language*, ed. J. Puhvel, pp. 163–81. Berkeley and Los Angeles: University of California Press.

Lambert, W. E., and Rawlings, C. 1969. Bilingual processing of mixed-language associative networks. *Journal of Verbal Learning and Verbal Behavior* 8: 604–9.

Lambert, W. E., and Tucker, G. R. 1972. *Bilingual education of children: The St. Lambert experiment.* Rowley, Mass.: Newbury House.

Lopez, M. 1977. Psycholinguistic research and bilingual education. In *Chicano psychology,* ed. J. Martinez, pp. 127–40. New York: Academic Press.

Lopez, M., Hicks, R. E., and Young, R. K. 1974. Retroactive inhibition in a bilingual A-B, A-B² paradigm. *Journal of Experimental Psychology* 103: 85–90.

Lopez, M., and Young, R. K. 1974. The linguistic interdependence of bilinguals. *Journal of Experimental Psychology* 102: 981–83.

MacNamara, J. 1967. The bilingual's linguistic performance: A psychological overview. *Journal of Social Issues* 8: 58–77.

Mehan, H., Cazden, C., Coles, L., Fisher, S., and Maroules, N. 1976. *The social organization of classroom lessons.* San Diego: Center for Human Information Processing Report, Dec. 1976, University of California.

Newby, R. W. 1976. Effects of bilingual language system on release from proactive inhibition. Southwestern Psychological Association, May.

Phillips, S. V. 1972. Participant structures and communicative competence: Warm Springs children in community classrooms. In *Functions of language in the classroom,* eds. Cazden, John, and Hymer, pp. 370–94. New York: Teachers College, Columbia University.

Price-Williams, D. R. 1976. *Explorations in cross-cultural psychology.* San Francisco, Cal.: Chandler and Sharp Publishers, Inc.

Ramírez III, M. 1977. Recognizing and understanding diversity: Multiculturalism and the Chicano movement in psychology. In *Chicano psychology,* ed. J. Martinez, pp. 343–54. New York: Academic Press.

Ramírez III, M., and Castañeda, A. 1974. *Cultural democracy, bicognitive development, and education.* New York: Academic Press.

Riegel, K. F. 1968. Some theoretical considerations of bilingual development. *Psychological Bulletin* 70: 674–76.

Rosansky, E. J. 1976. Methods and morphemes in second language acquisition research. *Language Learning* 26: 409–25.

Schacter, F. F., Kirshner, D., Dilps, B., Friedricks, M., and Sanders, K. 1974. *Everyday preschool interpersonal speech usage: Methodological, developmental and sociolinguistic studies.* Monographs of Society for Research on Child Development, vol. 39.

Slobin, D. I. 1975. On the nature of talk to children. In *Foundations of language development,* eds. E. Lenneberg and E. Lenneberg, pp. 284–96. London: UNESCO Press.

Snow, C. E. 1972. Mother's speech to children learning language. *Child development* 43: 549–65.

Snow, C. E., and Fergeson, C. 1977. *Mother's speech to children.* London: Oxford University Press.

Sorenson, A. P. 1967. Multilingualism in the Northwest Amazon. *American Anthropologist* 69: 670–84.

Spolsky, B. 1970. Navaho language maintenance: Six-year-olds in 1969. *Language Sciences* 13: 19–24.

Weinreich, U. 1953. *Languages in contact.* New York: Linguistic Circle of New York.

4

Language Transfer

Introduction

"Transfer or no transfer, that is the question." This statement succinctly accentuates one of the most controversial educational dilemmas in bilingual-bicultural education today. Several empirical and theoretical concerns converge on a central question: What is the influence of one language upon another during bilingual (or second language) acquisition? The psychological literature concerning itself with learning during the past two decades has reflected more than a simple interest in "learning set," "transfer of training," and "generalization." At a linguistic level, contrastive analysis proponents have at the same time concerned themselves with "competing linguistic structures," "semantic differentiation," and "error analysis." Most recent is the developmental psycholinguist's "developmental language errors" and "creative construction process." What each of these major conceptual emphases suggests is that transfer from one language to another continues to receive a great deal of research attention.

It is the function of the proposed discussion to provide a comprehensive and critical review of psychological, linguistic, and developmental conceptualizations relevant to bilingualism and the transfer phenomenon. Secondly, an attempt will be made to present empirical (descriptive and experimental) data related to this phenomenon. Lastly, an attempt will be made to relate conceptual, theoretical, and empirical information to teaching-learning strategies potentially relevant to bilingual-bicultural education classrooms. Because of the potential extensiveness of this topic, I will restrict myself to early childhood, a period easily identified as linguistically, psychologically, socially, and educationally significant.

Bilingualism Defined

For purposes of clarity, early childhood bilingualism will be defined within the boundaries of the following conditions.

Linguistic   Children are able to comprehend and/or produce some aspects of each language beyond the ability to discriminate that either one language or another is being spoken. This is not an extremely limiting condition since it allows many combinations of linguistic competence to fall within the boundaries of bilingualism. (The most "simple" to be included might be the child who has memorized one or more lexical utterances in a second language.)

Social   Children are exposed "naturally" to the two systems of languages as they are used in the form of social interaction during early childhood. This condition requires a substantive bilingual environment in the child's first three to five years of life. In many cases, this exposure comes from within a nuclear and extended family network, but this need not be the case (visitors and extended visits to foreign countries are examples of alternative environments).

Psychological-Developmental   The simultaneous character of development must be apparent in both languages. This is contrasted with the case in which a native speaker of one language who, after mastery of that language, begins on a course of second language acquisition.

These combined conditions define the present population of

interest. It is clear from this definition that an attempt is made to consider both the child's linguistic abilities and the social environment during an important psychological "segment" of life.

It is probably best to admit at this point that several theoretical formulations are presently available to account for the process and form of bilingual acquisition. McLaughlin (1977) best summarized the incongruencies in theoretical positions by admitting the unavailability of firm empirical information pertaining to second language acquisition. Such beliefs have been generated through extensions of previous work with children acquiring their native language and adults acquiring a second language. Only recently has a major research effort begun to emerge with children acquiring a second language during the ages of two to five. Therefore, it is not justifiable at present to provide an unclouded single view concerning this important developmental phenomenon. Instead, various views, each worthy of consideration, emerge. The following discussion is an attempt to bring these views into focus and critically assess their value.

Conceptualizations of Language Transfer

As previously indicated, one of the more interesting controversial and important issues related to early childhood bilingualism is the interactive influence of acquiring two languages across receptive and expressive domains. The phenomenon has traditionally been defined as language transfer, a term almost synonymous with language "interference." This term has gained multiple meanings with respect to bilingualism as is shown by its acquisition of several modifiers—"linguistic interference," "psychological interference," and "educational interference" (Saville 1971). Transfer within the present context will be defined as the influence of the acquisition and use of one language on the acquisition and the use of the other in the bilingual child.

Figure 4.1 presents a schematic of linguistic parameters operating during bilingual development. That is, any child who must deal with two languages must deal with the linguistic components represented in Figure 4.1. Two broad linguistic domains are represented in the two (L_1 and L_2) languages: a receptive domain and an expressive domain. Within each of these

Figure 4.1. An interactive description of bilingualism.

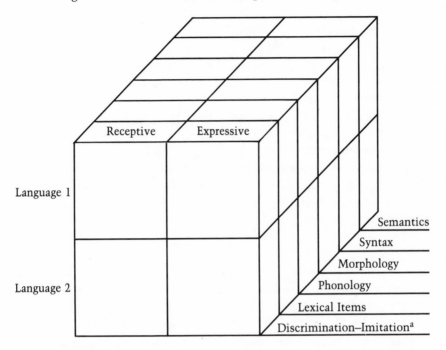

[a]This particular descriptive category relates only to the issue of comprehension (Receptive Speech). Expression in this case requires the ability of the subject to imitate, correctly, instances of each language.

domains, six linguistic parameters are represented: discrimination-imitation, lexicon, phonology, morphology, syntax, and semantics. Conceptually, then, it is possible to predict "linguistic transfer" within and between linguistic domains, and within and between linguistic parameters. Transfer is possible phonologically, morphologically, syntactically, semantically, within and across receptive and expressive domains.

Transfer might also occur at paralinguistic levels within the realm of intonation (accent), speed of articulation, and so on. Moreover, transfer could be evidenced by mixed-language utterances (El *horse* es mio), displacement ("forgetting" a term, etc.), and more severe general linguistic disorders (for example, stuttering, false starts, repeating, and so forth). To be frank, this notion of linguistic transfer is quite complex. It is important to note that the above possible transfer outcomes are presented here so as to indicate the complexity of the issue. It is not the case that empirical information is presently available to document the existence of these effects.

It is important also to indicate that transfer, as conceptually presented thus far, can act both positively and negatively. That is, language acquisition in one language can either be enhanced or diminished by acquisition and use of a second language. Too often, previous discussions of this phenomenon have failed to emphasize this duality. More specifically, "errors" in morphology, syntax, or semantics in one language may be related to transfer effects just as "nonerrors" in morphology, syntax, or semantics in one language may be related to transfer effects. These specific and general "possible" outcomes have led to a quandary concerning the acquisition of more than one language.

Second Language Acquisition

The study of second language acquisition must be considered here because of its applicability both theoretically and methodologically to the issue of bilingual acquisition. This form of research has been concerned with those variables operating in the acquisition of a second language after the native language has been acquired. Investigations of young children undergoing the process of second language acquisition have been completed only recently. Research in this area has borrowed extensively from the work in first language acquisition. That is, the same linguistic features have been of interest within the same methodological framework. Specifically, procedures for accumulating data on second language acquisition have taken on two forms: samples of spontaneous speech of the individual are gathered in his second language during periods of early, middle, and late exposure to the second language; and cross-sectional investigations of individuals exposed for varying amounts of time to the second language are undertaken. Typically, investigations of this nature make use of specific language measurement instruments designed to maximize the probability of the occurrence of certain linguistic forms.

Second language acquisition research has also made use of contrastive analysis. This technique calls for the comparative analysis of L_1 with L_2 so as to identify phonological, morphological, syntactic, and semantic differences and similarities (Stockwell and Bowen 1965). This form of analysis is used to predict the relative probability of linguistic transfer owing to the differences and similarities of L_1 and L_2. Therefore, if a speaker of Spanish is learning English, errors in adjective-noun syntactic placement may be frequent due to the differences in rules governing this syntagmatic relationship. On the other hand, plurals in Spanish and English are formed similarly by addition of an *s* or *es* inflection to singular noun. (This is an oversimplification, since there are other allomorphs in each language.) In this case, we might expect the L_2 learner to be able to transfer positively his past experiences with this morphological form owing to previous experiences with this inflectional derivative in L_1.

Dulay and Burt (1972) have utilized the above methodology to investigate the type of errors made by children who are learning second languages. This extensive research effort has made use of cross-sectional administration of a speech elicitation instrument, the Bilingual Syntax Measure (BSM), in order to study the development of specific morphological and syntactic forms. The BSM attempts to elicit production of target morphemes by combining the presentation of several cartoon pictures and strategic tester dialogue. Subjects' scores are determined by considering the number of utterances in which fully formed, partially correct morphemes are either present or absent in obligatory context. Morpheme order is determined by listing scores from highest percentage of occurrence to lowest percentage of occurrence. Rank orders such as these are used to compare morpheme development from one group of subjects (Spanish-speakers learning English) to a second group of subjects (Chinese-speakers learning English).

These studies with the BSM have led these researchers to make the following conclusions: There is an invariant order of acquisition among second language learners with respect to grammatical morphemes (as measured by the BSM). Fewer than 5 percent of all English errors are directly traceable to "interference" errors: errors related to L_1 forms. Children learn a second language via a creative construction process: "They gradually reconstruct rules for the speech they hear guided by a universal innate mechanism. . . ."

The theoretical and applied implications seem clear from these three conclusions. Theoretically, it would seem that L_2 acquisition is very much like L_1 acquisition. In fact, Dulay and Burt (1974), in a detailed analysis of the few errors that were observed during the BSM administration, assigned responsibility for those errors to the "creative construction process" rather than previous L_1 rule-governing experiences. That is, observed errors were more related to language learning rather than to the influence of L_1 and L_2 structures.

Several methodological and empirical considerations leave doubt in the conclusions drawn by the above researchers. First, the studies reported have used a technique of considerable questionability with respect to linguistic measurement. The BSM is designed to elicit particular morpheme constructions under semicontrolled testing situations. It does not allow the gathering of a "natural" language sample. The influence of "demand" characteristics posed by the testing of stimuli and the multitude of administration variables has been documented experimentally (Mercer 1973). LoCoco (1976), in a comparative study of typical methods of data collection of L_2 data ("natural" versus "standardized"), presents evidence indicating the differential influences of these methods on the number of specific L_2 errors. In addition, Hakuta (1974) has reported a different morpheme-acquisition order than reported by Dulay and Burt. His investigations considered the acquisition of English in a Japanese five year old.

Rosansky (1976) detailed particular L_1 effects on L_2 acquisition for Spanish-speaking children and adults acquiring English. The data strongly suggest that morpheme-acquisition order in L_2 is related to L_1 morpheme similarities. Moreover, in a detailed comparative study of L_2 acquisition using several language assessment techniques, including the BSM, Larson-Freeman (1976) and Porter (1977) found differences in morpheme orders of acquisition with other measures excluding the BSM. Given these series of empirical results, it is impossible to conclude that an invariant ordering of morphemes now occurs during L_2 acquisition (see Bailey, Madden, and Krashen 1974; Larson-Freeman 1976; Rosansky 1976, for a more detailed review of L_2 acquisition).

Even more recent is the work of Mace-Matluck (1979) who reports a comparative study of five- to ten-year-old Spanish, Cantonese, and Hakano-speaking children who were learning

English as a second language. Specifically, she has reported that the rank orders of morpheme development obtained with the use of the MAT-SEA-CAL Oral Proficiency Test (Matluck and Mace-Matluck 1974) did not correlate significantly with Brown's (1973) L_1 sequence for English monolingual children. Moreover, she reports: Rank orders obtained for children who speak non-Indo European languages showed lower correspondence with the L_1 sequence (Mace-Matluck 1979: 79).

Bilingual Acquisition

As indicated previously, transfer might be considered both general and specific in nature. That is, it is possible that the requirements imposed on a child with respect to multilingual acquisition would lead to a general linguistic lag compared to a child whose communicative requirements center on one distinct language. Carrow's (1971, 1972) work concerning the measurement of receptive abilities for three- to seven-year-old Spanish-English bilinguals and English monolinguals is relevant to this notion of general "interference." Measures across languages indicated that English developed faster than Spanish for bilingual children and that English for these same bilinguals was lower than English for monolingual age controls. This English lag was evident during early ages (three to five years) but not at later ages (six to seven years). Although these data suggest a possible causal relationship between bilingualism and the initial "rate" of language acquisition, it is far from conclusive. In fact, Padilla and Liebman (1975) report contradictory evidence. Their analysis of two three-year-old bilingual children's linguistic development suggested no general language lag in either language. By comparing these subjects' utterances to those reported by González (1970) for monolingual Spanish children, they were able to conclude:

There is no evidence in the language samples that might suggest an overall reduced or slower rate of language growth for the bilingual children of other studies (p. 51).

Because the notion of a general lag does not consider the possible importance of specific language form similarities and differences, it does not seem to hold much promise for identifying important levels of interaction operating during bilingual acquisition. Therefore, a more specific analysis of linguistic interaction which considers such differences and similarities is necessary.

Experimental studies of specific instances of "transfer" or lack of it are available with bilingual children. For instance, Evans (1974) reports a comparison of word-pair discriminations and word imitations in Spanish and English for monolingual English and bilingual Spanish/English children. Elementary schoolchildren were asked to discriminate between words containing English sounds considered difficult for Spanish-speakers. (Examples are the phonemes /b/ and /v/ which are clearly separate in English but not so clearly in Spanish.) Additionally, children were requested to imitate a series of words in each language that have this same "difficult" characteristic. Bilinguals did not differ from monolinguals on all English tasks.

García and Trujillo (1979) report a similar finding when they compared bilingual (Spanish/English) and monolingual (English) three, four, five, six, and seven year olds on high-error-risk phonemes (phonemes in Spanish that adult Spanish-speakers mispronounce), and simple-to-complex syntactic forms (sentences containing plural and possessive morphemes). Bilinguals did not differ from monolinguals on English imitation tasks (where both groups scored near 100 percent correct) but they did differ significantly (made less errors) than English-speakers on Spanish tasks. This was the case at all age levels. These studies suggest that negative transfer at the phonological level in young bilingual children is nonexistent.

In this same study (García and Trujillo 1979), however, the imitation of complex Spanish sentences which involved adjective placement were not imitated correctly by the bilingual subjects. Complex English sentences of this type presented no significant problem for either bilingual or English-only children. Recall that adjective placement in Spanish ("pato *azul*") differs from that in English ("*blue* duck"). Therefore, it is likely that transfer (both positive and/or negative) is a possibility as syntactic complexity increases and as differences in syntactic structure between the languages of the bilingual are involved.

Interlanguage Transfer: A Developmental Analysis

In a recent study, we attempted to evaluate the effect of native language negative constructions on the production of second language negative syntactic forms.

Three-, four-, and five-year-old Spanish-English bilingual children participated in a task which required them to describe productively "negation" relationships portrayed for them using common toys (cars with and without wheels, and so forth). These children were requested to perform this task in Spanish and English. Additionally, monolingual children of the same age groupings were given these tasks in English. In this manner, an analysis of the development of negation was possible for both bilingual and monolingual children as well as a comparative analysis of the character of that development between these two linguistic groups.

Tables 1–6 present graphically and summarily the results of the study. The mean percentage of correct negative agent-verb sequences in Spanish was 100 percent for all groups (see Tables 4.1, 4.2, and 4.3). Moreover, bilinguals did not include *hacer* or *do* forms in their Spanish negative constructions across all age groups. Bilingual subjects' performance in English seemed to reflect Spanish language constructions. The mean percentage of correct negative-verb sequence increased with the age of the subject. Bilinguals "correctly" omitted subjects in Spanish constructions and also tended "incorrectly" to omit subjects in English negative constructions. For four year olds, 35 percent of negative constructions included subjects. Five and six year olds included subjects in approximately 15 percent and 50 percent of their negative constructions, respectively. In addition, bilinguals had a lower frequency of *do*'s in their English negative constructions (see Tables 4.4, 4.5, and 4.6).

Monolinguals consistently performed at higher levels on the three dependent measures, except at age five for *do* inclusions at which point bilinguals seemed to demonstrate a higher frequency of *do* inclusions (see Tables 4.2, 4.5, 4.6). The mean percentage of correct negative-verb sequence was high for English monolinguals, from approximately 71 percent for three year olds, up to 100 percent for six year olds (Table 4.4). Monolinguals also had a significantly higher frequency of subject inclusion in their

TABLE 4.1

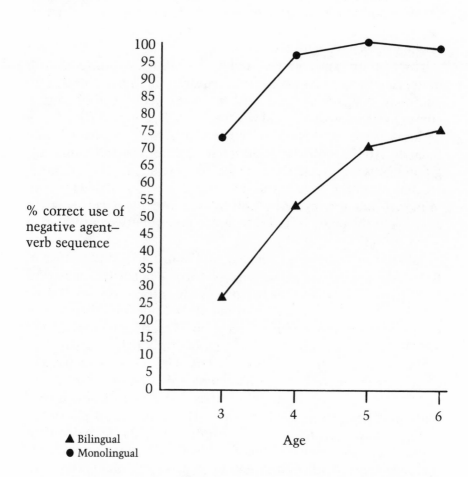

% correct use of negative agent–verb sequence

▲ Bilingual
● Monolingual

Age

negative constructions (Table 4.5). This contrast in findings between bilingual and monolingual groups seems to suggest the influence of Spanish on English negative constructions. In addition, monolinguals consistently included a significantly higher proportion of *do*'s in their negative constructions than did bilinguals (Table 4.6). Interestingly, there seemed to be a crossover at five years of age in which bilinguals produced a higher frequency of do's than did monolinguals.

Conspicuously absent from the present data is any apparent demonstration of a "complete" transfer effect between languages. A transfer hypothesis predicts that language interaction is a re-

TABLE 4.2

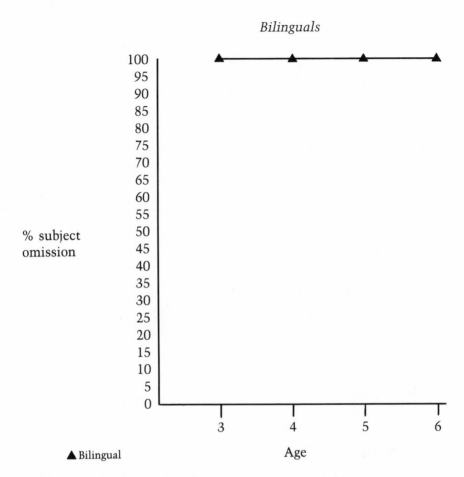

Bilinguals

% subject
omission

▲ Bilingual   Age

ciprocal process, but the present data reveal only that "correct" English use reflected Spanish language intrusion. Performance with Spanish negative constructions in the three dependent measures remained high at 100 percent correct. Cummins (1979) suggests that if a bilingual child attains only a low level of competence in a first or second language, then interaction with the environment through that language, both in terms of input and output, is likely to be impoverished. It seems appropriate at this point to suggest a selective language-transfer phenomenon since bilinguals did produce correct Spanish negative constructions which reflected, syntactically, Spanish construction gram-

Chapter 4

TABLE 4.3

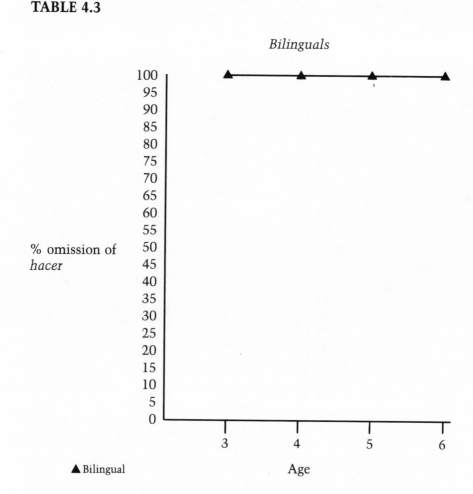

Bilinguals

% omission of *hacer*

▲ Bilingual

Age

mars. In the same manner the *do* support transformation which exists for English negative constructions was observed in high frequency with monolingual subjects of all ages. This transformational strategy does not exist in Spanish. Performance with Spanish constructions across the three dependent variables did not reflect English negative constructions which would be predicted by a transfer hypothesis. Certain statements about the relationship between the present findings and previous data seem worthy of considering. García (1977) reported that the acquisition of Spanish prepositions by three- and four-year-old English monolinguals resulted in an increase of incorrect English prep-

TABLE 4.4

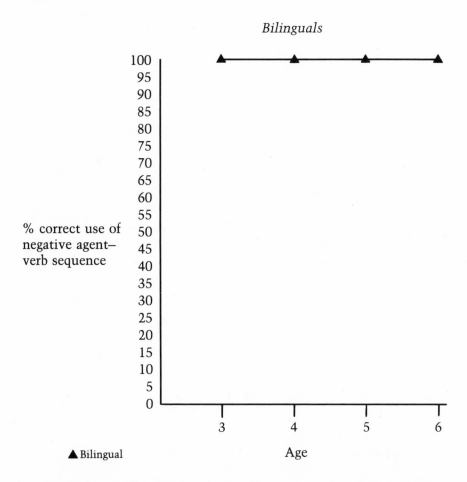

ositional use. This type of interaction, which was restricted to the expressive level, reflected the changes in one language which were related to changes in a second language. Butterworth (1972), in a report on the English development of a thirteen-year-old Colombian boy, found that sentence subjects were deleted; a deletion is permissible in Colombian Spanish. The results of the present study were consistent with Butterworth's findings.

The present evidence does not support Dulay and Burt's (1974) findings in which they report a very low percentage of linguistic errors in children learning English as a second language. Quite the opposite, the present data suggest that for negative syntactic

TABLE 4.5

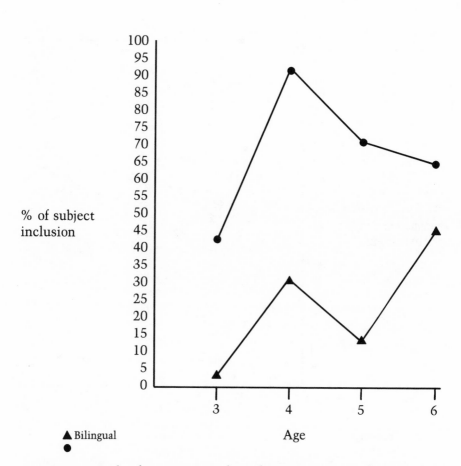

% of subject
inclusion

▲ Bilingual
●

Age

construction, the frequency and qualitative nature of errors for
bilinguals versus monolinguals are a reflection of previously acquired linguistic strategies. The present findings support a modified transfer hypothesis. A transfer theory predicts that new
constructions in a second language will reflect previously acquired construction strategies already formed during native language learning. This is supported by the findings of the present
research in which the negative-verb constructions were incorporated into English negative constructions. This was also the
case for phrase subject omission and *do* constructions.

This experiment represents a developmental strategy which

TABLE 4.6

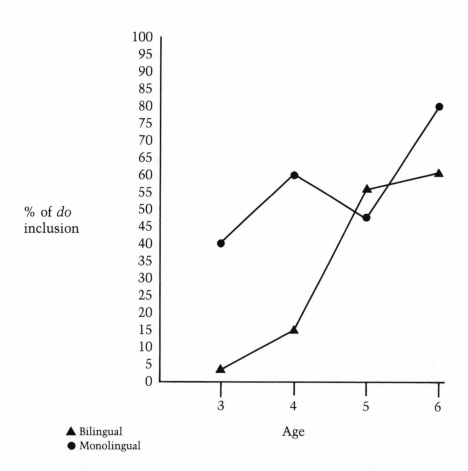

compared monolingual and bilingual subjects across specific linguistic categories represented in Figure 1. Such studies are meant
to test empirically a specific "interference" hypothesis during
early childhood bilingual acquisition. Yet, these cross-sectional,
as well as longitudinal, studies allow only correlational, not causal,
relationships to be identified. As Ervin-Tripp (1973) suggests,
"interference" in these samples is exemplified by performance
errors in the learner's linguistic system as they relate to a contrastive analysis of both languages involved. These investigations
require one major assumption: any identifiable "error" is causally

related to an interaction effect of the two identified languages. Unfortunately, this assumption is in need of empirical verification. For instance, linguistic observations of a young child may produce the following utterances: "¿Did you see *ese* carro?" or "*El* boy is going with us." Given our previous guide, each of these might be considered an example of interference. Yet a closer analysis of the child's total system might indicate that this type of linguistic format is his only model (it is not a function of the child's languages acting upon each other). Therefore, it would seem totally inappropriate to consider these utterances forms or symptoms of transfer.

Given the above methodological problems, it would seem more appropriate to consider the interactive nature of languages for the bilingual as linguistic transfer or generalization instead of "interference." Transfer has traditionally been used to indicate the effects of previous training experiences on present training experiences as it relates to specific learning tasks. Ellis (1972) summarized five factors that influence the transfer of learning between tasks: task similarity, time interval between tasks, degree of original learning, variety of previously learned tasks, and task difficulty. With respect to bilingual acquisition, research concentrating on transfer effects must consider more than the general error productions of children as they relate to a general contrastive analysis of the two languages involved. Additionally, this transfer analysis must be made available in both directions. The form of the question might be as follows: "How does present language learning affect new language learning and how does language learning affect previously learned language forms?" This question must be addressed in each language both from a positive and negative perspective. This strategy requires knowing present structures in each language, then tracking these and future language changes so as to make a correlational analysis available for inspection.

Since it may be difficult to assess all these training variables, it may be of theoretical and empirical importance to consider the interactive effects of bilingualism during acquisition as a special case of generalization. Generalization is a more functional construct which links nonmanipulated dependent variable changes to manipulated independent variable changes. Therefore, this phenomenon would concentrate on those changes in one language which occur as a function of changes in the second language. For research purposes, this conceptualization calls for an experimental strategy requiring the manipulation of one language while concomitantly measuring the effect of that change on the second language.

Interlanguage Transfer: An Experimental Analysis

This methodology is best exemplified by a recent experiment which will be described in some detail here. The experiment investigated the effect of English language acquisition on already existing Spanish language forms with young (three- to four-year-old) children who came from bilingual home environments.

The present study attempted to provide an experimental analysis of two specific second language training strategies. One strategy (Independent L_1 and L_2 Training) introduces training in a second language without regard for first language maintenance. The second strategy (Simultaneous L_1 and L_2 Training) introduces training in a second language while at the same time providing a maintenance procedure for the first language. Subjects were children from Spanish-English bilingual home environments who indicated a high level of expressive competence on prepositional labels in Spanish (L_1) but not English (L_2). Training was introduced on prepositional labels in L_1. In this way, the effect (both direction and form) of training/learning a second language was provided during the training of second language prepositional labels. These manipulations provide a laboratory examination of much debated "second language" versus "maintenance" teaching procedure of interest to second language and bilingual instructors.

Subjects and Experimental Stimuli　　Four Mexican-American children, ranging in age from four years, three months to four years, eight months, all from bilingual, Spanish-English home environments, served as subjects. These children were bilingual kindergarten students in a local school district. Teacher and parent questionnaires indicated that these children were capable of speaking and understanding both Spanish and English but were judged as "Spanish-dominant."

The experimental stimuli consisted of black and white plastic

TABLE 4.7

Experimental Stimuli

English	Spanish
The cat on the table	El gato arriba de la mesa
The cat behind the table	El gato detrás de la mesa
The cat on the bed	El gato arriba de la cama
The cat behind the bed	El gato detrás de la cama
The cat on the chair[a]	El gato arriba de la silla[a]
The cat behind the chair[a]	El gato detrás de la silla[a]
The cat under the chair[a]	El gato debajo de la silla[a]
The cat in front of the chair[a]	El gato adelante de la silla[a]

[a]Probe items

drawings (4″ × 5½″) representing four positional concepts—on *(arriba de)*, behind *(detrás de)*, in front *(adelante de)*, and under *(abajo de)*, taken from the Northwestern Syntax Screening Test. A description of each card is presented in Table 4.7.

Pretests   Pretests were administered to each subject to determine linguistic ability in Spanish and English prior to any experimental manipulation. These pretests made use of the probe items identified in Table 4.7. (Prior to any pretest, all subjects were asked to point to items portrayed in the pictures to ensure their linguistic labeling skills with respect to these items. Responding on these trials necessitated a 100-percent-correct response criterion prior to pretesting.) All pretests contained both Spanish and English trials, randomly distributed. On receptive pretest trials, the experimenter instructed the subject in either Spanish or English to point to one of our specific cards depicting exemplars of *in, on, behind,* and *under.* Expressive pretest trials consisted of displaying a specific card and asking the position of an item (a cat) displayed on the card. Each began by displaying the card and asking, "Where is the cat? Is he *behind, under, in front of,* or *on* the chair?" or "¿Dónde está el gato? ¿Esta *detrás de, debajo de, adelante de,* o *arriba de* la silla?" (Note that two additional prepositions were included to increase the potential

TABLE 4.8

Order of Preposition Training by Subject

	Training Phases		
Subjects	A	B	C
	Independent L₂ Training		

Subjects	A	B	C
	Independent L_2 Training		
1	behind	on	behind/on
2	on	behind	on/behind
	Simultaneous L_1 and L_2 Training		
3	behind	on	behind/on
4	on	behind	on/behind

range of response.) The order of presentation for prepositions on each trial was random. The experimenter did not correct or deliver consequences for subject responses. A pretest of receptive trials was administered on the first day of the study and was followed by a pretest of expressive trials on the second day. Each of the four children selected for inclusion in this study responded at 100-percent levels in Spanish and 0 percent in English during pretest sessions.

Training Phases

After pretesting, two subjects were assigned to two separate second language training groups: Independent L_2 Training, and, Simultaneous L_1 and L_2 Training. The first two training phases for each subject represented training on one English prepositional label. (The training order for the two prepositions was counterbalanced between subjects in each group.) A third phase was included in which both labels received training simultaneously. Presented in Table 4.8 is a summary of prepositional labels trained during separate phases for each subject.

Independent L_2 Training   Subjects 1 and 2 were assigned to this training phase. During training trials, the subject was shown one of two training cards depicting an example of the preposition(s) included in the training session. Each trial was begun by placing the card(s) in front of the subject. The experimenter then pointed to the card being shown and asked "Where is the cat?" If the subject did not respond after ten seconds or responded incorrectly, the subject was asked to repeat an experimenter's corrected response. After correctly imitated responses, as well as correct responses to the initial question, subjects received verbal approval ("good," and so forth). Twenty-four training trials were included in each training session. During simultaneous training of the two prepositional labels (training phase C), an equal number of training trials (twelve) for each preposition was presented randomly within each training session.

Simultaneous L_1 and L_2 Training   For subjects 3 and 4, the training procedure was similar to that described above except that half of the training trials were in Spanish. Training trials were presented randomly in the languages with the constraint that no three consecutive training trials were in one language. All training was accomplished by a Mexican-American, Spanish-English, bilingual female experimenter.

Generalization Probes

After each training session, subjects were exposed to an additional thirty-two trials with the same experimenter. The probe pictures were used during these trials. Each probe picture was presented four times with a Spanish instruction requesting its label, and four times with an English instruction requesting its label. Probe cards for *on* and *behind* portrayed examples of these prepositions which utilized different objects than those in training cards. (Use of this procedure allowed a measure of prepositional response which was generalized in nature, that is, to pictures different from those used during training.) Termination of a training phase was determined by a probe session criterion of two consecutive sessions of 100 percent response on the preposition(s) being taught.

After the completion of a training phase, subjects were administered a receptive probe session. Procedures during this session were the same as those during the receptive pretest. This pro-

Figure 4.2.

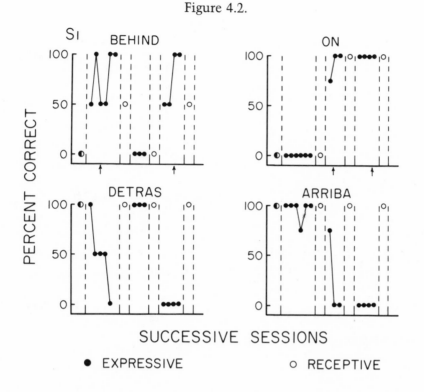

SUCCESSIVE SESSIONS

● EXPRESSIVE   ○ RECEPTIVE

cedure was included in order to monitor any changes in the subject's receptive response as a result of expressive training.

The exact verbal response was tape-recorded so as to allow a further qualitative analysis of incorrect responding. Interobserver scoring agreement was assessed for all pretest sessions and for 50 percent of training and probe sessions distributed throughout the study (at least one probe session for each phase). Agreement on a session basis was 100 percent for receptive trials and ranged from 96 to 100 percent for expressive trials.

Training Results   Although training results are not graphically presented, each subject reached near 100 percent correct response during each separate prepositional training phase on the preposition(s) being taught. Probe results are presented in Figures 4.2 to 4.5. These figures present percentage of correct response for both receptive and expressive trials during pretest-

Figure 4.3.

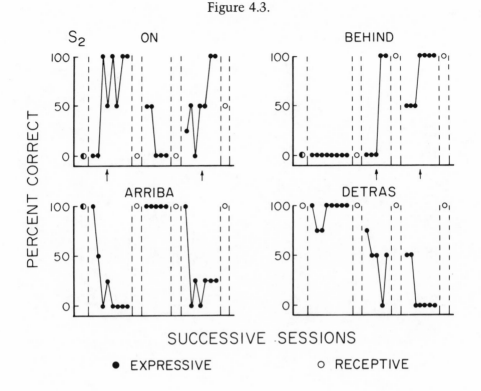

SUCCESSIVE SESSIONS

● EXPRESSIVE   ○ RECEPTIVE

ing and for successive probe sessions of the study for S_1–S_4, respectively.

Independent L_2 Training Results   During pretesting S_1 and S_2 responded at 100 percent correct in Spanish (L_1) and 0 percent correct in English (L_2). When L_2 training was introduced on the first preposition, correct responding on L_2 expressive probes increased from near 0 to 100 percent. During this same training phase, correct L_1 expressive response on the same prepositional concept decreased from 100 percent to near zero. This same phenomenon occurred when training on the second preposition was instituted in L_2. Moreover, correct response on the first prepositional concept returned to pretesting during this second training phase. Simultaneous training of the two L_2 prepositional labels produced correct response in L_2 and a decreased level of correct response in L_1.

Figure 4.4.

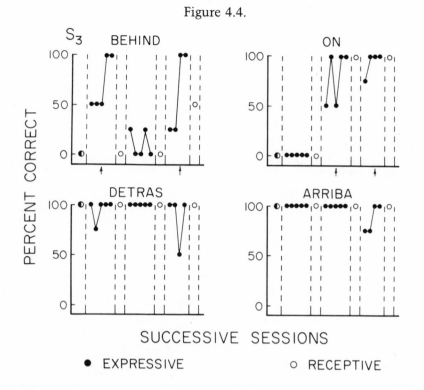

SUCCESSIVE SESSIONS

● EXPRESSIVE   ○ RECEPTIVE

During receptive pretesting for these same subjects, L_1 response was at 100 percent, while L_2 receptive response was at 0 percent. L_1 receptive response remained at 100 percent throughout the study, while L_2 response fluctuated between 0 and 100 percent, with variability between the two prepositional labels being taught.

A qualitative analysis of subject expressive response was performed by assessing the forms of subject errors on expressive probe trials. Almost all response errors (82–100 percent of errors in each session) were of a language-substitution type. That is, during L_2 training, L_1 labeling errors took the form of conceptually correct L_2 productions (for example, *detrás* for *behind*).

Simultaneous L_1 and L_2 Training Results   Results for S_3 and S_4 contrast those effects identified for S_1 and S_2 on expressive probes. As correct response on L_2 probe trials increased for each

Figure 4.5

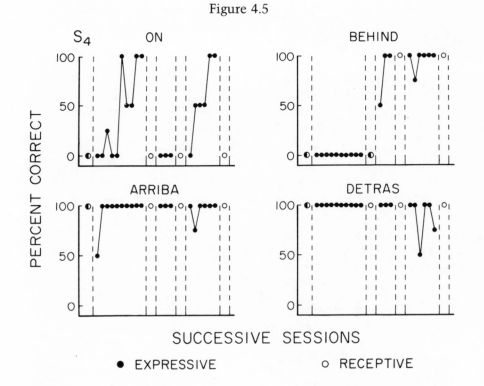

SUCCESSIVE SESSIONS

● EXPRESSIVE   ○ RECEPTIVE

preposition trained, there was not a corresponding decrease in correct L_1 probe trial response. That is, during the time correct response in L_2 prepositions increased to 100 percent, correct response on L_1 prepositions remained at or near 100 percent. Response on receptive probes was consistently 100 percent for L_1 and variable for L_2. For S_3 an increase in correct response from 0 to 50 percent for *behind* and from 0 to 100 percent for *on* was observed. For S_4, an increase from 0 to 100 percent for *behind* was observed, while no change in correct response was observed for *on*.

A qualitative analysis of subject expressive response was performed by assessing the form of subject errors on expressive probes. Almost all response errors (90–100 percent of error in each session) were in L_2. Subjects responded to the L_2 instruction in the preposition that had previously been being taught. For example, if *detrás/behind* was taught, subjects responded *behind* on L_2 probe trials. Spanish errors were almost non-existent. Probe results are not presented graphically for probe trials depicting *in (en)* and *under (debajo de)*. Correct response in these probe trials remained consistent: near 100 percent in Spanish and near 0 percent in English.

The present study has suggested an experimental analysis of language transfer in young children. By manipulating linguistic response in one language (L_2) and monitoring effects of this manipulation in another language (L_1), a cause-effect analysis between language interaction was attempted during specific language training interventions. The results of this study indicate that expressive acquisition of prepositional labels in L_2 occurred; that this acquisition led to a distinct change in the expressive use of the corresponding prepositional label in L_1 during the Independent L_2 Training; that this change was characterized by L_2 substitutions for occasions calling for L_1 response; that no such effect occurred during a Simultaneous L_1 and L_2 Training; and that no such effect was observed for receptive response. (Some increase was actually observed in receptive L_2 response.) Therefore, children taught to respond only in L_2 failed to discriminate the appropriate use of L_1 and L_2 prepositional labeling. Those children receiving training trials in both L_1 and L_2 made the appropriate discrimination.

During Independent L_2 Training, a form of linguistic substitution was identified. This substitution may very well reflect the relative exposure to the two languages during this condition (Riegel 1968). It may also reflect the sociolinguistic character of the training setting (Gumperz and Hernandez 1972) or the occurrence of such an effect in bilingual children where a "dominance" in Spanish exists. The present study is unable to support or eliminate these and possible other alternative explanations. Even so, a clear transfer effect was produced in this learning situation. Dulay and Burt (1974) have failed to find any large-scale evidence for such effects in the speech of children acquiring a second language. The present data suggest that the form of such effects and the conditions under which they occur may be diverse. That is, transfer may take on the form of language substitution under certain environmental conditions within which L_2 acquisition occurs. It is important to note that the character of the present experimentally identified effects (language substitution) may not be identifiable in narrative studies (or, if identified, might be considered code switching).

For Simultaneous L_1 and L_2 Training, expressive training results indicated a rapid acquisition of "new" language prepositions. In addition, no "negative transfer" effects were identified. That is, subjects responded correctly to Spanish prepositions undergoing training during posttraining probe sessions, while continuing to respond at a consistently high level (near 100 percent) in English. As each training phase was completed, correct response for the Spanish preposition undergoing training increased. The differential response at the expressive level between Independent and Simultaneous Training was an important factor in decreasing the previous generalization ("transfer") effects.

With respect to language-teaching strategies, it seems appropriate to suggest that language training programs with bilingual children consider the relationship of the two languages within the training context. In this study, generalized effects which might be termed "substitution" in L_1 were observed within a training that emphasized only L_2. During training which emphasized both L_1 and L_2, no such linguistic disruption on L_1 was observed.

In summary, this study, although preliminary in nature, provides a methodology for experimental analysis of language-transfer effects. It also demonstrates that by taking the character of training into account (presenting trained instances of both languages during training), first language disruptions in the form of language substitution (failure to discriminate the appropriate use of L_1 or L_2) were significantly reduced. Further research in this area must concentrate on more complex morphological and syntactic forms and also must consider the influence of the present independent variable outside the confines of laboratory situations.

Summary of Empirical Evidence

The studies in the field of linguistic transfer with young bilingual children can be used to support one or more of the following contradictory conclusions concerning the acquisition of two languages during early childhood:

1. The developmental character of the bilingual is not signif-

icantly influenced by the simultaneous linguistic development of two languages; the development of character of each language is similar to that of a native speaker of either language.

2. A linguistic transfer phenomenon is evident in which the specific structures of the dominant language influence the developmental quality of the less dominant language.

3. A linguistic transfer phenomenon is evident in which the structure of the less dominant language influences the quality of the dominant language, under "learning" conditions which emphasize the "learning" of the less-dominant language without regard to the maintenance of the dominant language.

Given the contradictory nature of the evidence available at this time, it is safest to conclude that the specific character of transfer between the languages of the bilingual continues to be an area of significant research interest and controversy. It would be inappropriate at this time to make any other conclusion.

Specific Implications for Early Childhood Education

It is always difficult to extract from a body of research literature specific implications for an applied teaching technology. The character of controlled research environment, the uncharacteristic control of intervening variables, and the starchiness of independent variable intervention often preclude generalization of findings to "real" classrooms. McLaughlin's (1978) review of such research led him to conclude that many misconceptions are prevalent with respect to language and bilingual acquisition in early childhood:

1. The young child acquires a language more quickly and easily than an adult because the child is biologically programmed to acquire language whereas the adult is not.
2. The younger the child, the more skilled in acquiring a second language.
3. Second language acquisition is a qualitatively different process than first language acquisition.
4. Interference between first and second language is an inevitable and ubiquitous part of second language acquisition.
5. There is a single method of second language instruction that is most effective with all children.
6. The experience of bilingualism negatively (or positively) affects

the child's intellectual development, language skills, educational attainment, emotional adjustment, and/or cognitive functioning.
(McLaughlin 1978: 197–205)

McLaughlin is not admitting total ignorance in concluding that the above propositions are false. Instead, he is following the strategy of any good scientist: propositions which are extracted from empirical observation and experimentation are to be handled with extreme caution. It is possible that some or all of the above propositions are true, but to claim their truth, at a time when empirical support is unavailable, is clearly not in the best interest of future research and the applied technology of education.

Is it possible to address any bilingual education concerns? With the above caution in mind, there are some questions specifically related to bilingual education in early childhood which deserve discussion.

Will bilingual education efforts in early childhood negatively affect children's linguistic development?   Given the data discussed previously, it seems clear that exposure to two language systems and subsequent proficiency in these two languages does not retard linguistic development. That is, children who were operating at complex levels in Spanish were not retarded in English as compared to other matched monolingual English-speaking children. Therefore, a bilingual experience in early childhood alone does not necessarily retard linguistic development. Unfortunately, important questions still remain: How are differences in the qualitative nature of the bilingual experience related to linguistic development? How are cognitive process variables related to bilingual development?

Do bilingual education efforts in early childhood positively influence linguistic development?   Although there is evidence for the lack of negative effects of bilingual acquisition on general development, there is no evidence of advanced linguistic development for bilinguals when compared to matched monolinguals. That is, there is no report of bilingual subjects' increased ability in either language as compared to native monolingual speakers of either language. Cognitively, evidence exists that bilinguals score significantly higher on several cognitive measures than matched monolingual peers (Cummins 1979). These measures tend to be those reflecting the ability to consider properties of the environment in a more flexible manner: to construct more general semantic categories than monolingual peers. Critical questions remain, however: Are these advantages related to bilingualism or other (potentially cultural) variables associated with bilingualism? Are these advantages related to proficiency levels of bilingualism? If so, what is linguistic proficiency? Are these advantages related to the specific languages involved and specific cognitive measures (tasks)?

Should bilingual education efforts in early childhood be immersion, transition-ESL, or transition-maintenance? There is very little evidence on which to base even the most cautious answers to this question. Certainly, previous immersion efforts have been evaluated positively for elementary schoolchildren in French-English schools of Canada (Lambert and Tucker 1972). A similar conclusion for Spanish-English elementary schoolchildren in the United States is not warranted. Recall that prior to the formal funding of bilingual education at the national level in 1968, the English immersion program was the model for the education of language minority children in the United States public schools. That program has proven disastrous for these children (Carter 1970).

Data from empirical efforts in bilingual and cognitive development shed some light on this question. Dulay and Burt (1972, 1974), based on the low incidence of second language errors related to native language structure, have suggested that incidental teaching of a second language might prove most beneficial. That is, an immersion or transition effort which allows the child to be exposed to the second language as naturally as possible without formal language instruction seems the most effective strategy for second language acquisition. Data presented previously in this manuscript suggest that a formal maintenance instruction system which reinforces the native language and at the same time formally teaches a second language produces a parallel development in both languages. Cummins (1979) reviews several studies which indicate that cognitive flexibility is an attribute of only the proficient bilingual. Monolinguals and unbalanced bilinguals scored significantly lower on Piagetian and traditional tests of cognitive development than did proficient preschool bilinguals. Therefore, transition-maintenance bilingual efforts may enhance both acquisition of new language structures and provide advantageous cognitive benefits. Of course, sound evaluation of immersion, transition, and maintenance bilingual programs in early childhood are needed prior to any (even cautious) conclusions concerning whether the adequacy or relative effectiveness of these strategies is possible. Still remaining are the other curriculum questions: Should languages be temporally and contextually separated? (E.g., teacher A speaks L_1, teacher B speaks L_2; Monday and Friday, L_1, Tuesday and Thursday, L_2.) Should content areas be repeated in both languages? What is the role of translation as a curricular tool?

In conclusion, it remains difficult to speculate on the implications of bilingual research in the area of linguistic transfer for bilingual education in early childhood. It does seem clear that bilingual experiences need not produce negative effects. Beyond such a general conclusion, more specific conclusions have been extracted from the research literature within each section of this manuscript. Unfortunately, more questions than answers have been generated by the research community. This is not as discouraging as it might seem, for it is challenges like those ahead in early childhood bilingual education that will undoubtedly provide benefits for all children who must acquire the language(s) of their society(ies) during early childhood.

References

Bailey, N., Madden, L., and Krashen, S. 1974. Is there a "natural sequence" in adult second language learning? *Language Learning* 24: 233–43.

Brown, R. A. 1973. *A first language: The early stages.* Cambridge, Mass.: Harvard University Press.

Butterworth, G. 1972. A Spanish-speaking adolescent's acquisition of English syntax. M.A. thesis, University of California at Los Angeles.

Carrow, E. 1971. Comprehension of English and Spanish by preschool Mexican-American children. *Modern Language Journal* 55: 299–306.

———. 1972. Auditory comprehension of English by monolingual and bilingual preschool children. *Journal of Speech and Hearing Research* 15: 407–57.

Carter, T. 1970. *Mexican Americans in school: A history of educational neglect.* New York: College Entrance Examination Board.

Cummins, J. 1979. Linguistic interdependence and the educational development of bilingual children. *Review of Educational Research* 49: 22–251.

Dulay, H. C., and Burt, M. K. 1972. Goofing: An indication of children's second language learning strategies. *Language Learning* 22: 235–52.

———. 1974. A new perspective on the creative construction in child second language acquisition. *Language Learning* 24: 253–78.

Ellis, H. C. 1972. *Fundamentals of human learning and cognition.* Dubuque, Iowa: W. C. Brown Co.

Ervin-Tripp, S. 1973. *Language acquisition and communicative choice.* Stanford, Calif.: Stanford University Press.

Evans, J. S. 1974. Word-pair discrimination and imitation abilities of preschool Spanish-speaking children. *Journal of Learning Disabilities* 7: 573–84.

García, E. 1977. The study of early childhood bilingualism: Strategies for linguistic transfer research. In *Chicano Psychology,* ed. J. L. Martinez, Jr., pp. 141–54. New York: Academic Press.

García, E., and Trujillo, A. 1979. A developmental comparison of English and Spanish imitation between bilingual and monolingual children. *Journal of Educational Psychology* 21: 161–68.

González, G. 1970. The acquisition of Spanish grammar by native Spanish speakers. Ph.D. dissertation, University of Texas.

Gumperz, J. J., and Hernandez, E. 1972. Bilingualism, bidialectism, and classroom interaction. In *The function of language in the classroom,* eds. C. Cazden, V. P. John and D. Hymes, pp. 164–82. New York: Teachers College Press.

Hakuta, K. 1974. Prefabricated patterns and the emergence of structure in second language acquisition. *Language Learning* 24: 287–97.

Holguin, R. 1977. *Curriculum and instruction: A handbook for teaching in a bilingual setting.* Pomona: Multilingual Multicultural Materials Development Center.

Kolers, P. A. 1968. Bilingualism and information processing. *Scientific American* 218: 78–89.

Lambert, W., and Tucker, G. 1972. *Bilingual education of children: The St. Lambert experiment.* Rowley, Mass.: Newbury House.

Larson-Freeman, D. 1976. An explanation for the morpheme acquisition order of second language learners. *Language Learning* 26: 125–34.

Lo Coco, V. 1976. A comparison of three methods for collection of L_2 data: Free composition, translation and picture description. *Working Papers on Bilingualism* 8: 59–86.

Lopez, M., Hicks, R. E., and Young, R. K. 1974. Retroactive inhibition in a bilingual A-B, A-B[1] paradigm. *Journal of Experimental Psychology* 102: 85–90.

Lopez, M., and Young, R. K. 1974. The linguistic interdependence of bilinguals. *Journal of Experimental Psychology* 102: 981–83.

Mace-Matluck, B. J. 1979. The order of acquisition of English structures by Spanish speaking children: Some possible determinants. In *The acquisition and use of Spanish and English as 1st and 2nd languages*, ed. R. W. Anderson, pp. 78–87. Washington, D.C.: TESOL.

Matluck, J. H., and Mace-Matluck, B. J. 1974. *MAT-SEA-CAL oral proficiency tests: English, Spanish, Cantonese, Mandarin, Tagalog, Ilokano.* Arlington, Va.: Center for Applied Linguistics.

McLaughlin, B. 1977. Second-language acquisition in childhood. *Psychological Bulletin* 84: 438–59.

———. 1978. *Second language acquisition in childhood.* Hillsdale, N.J.: Lawrence Erlbaum Assoc., Inc.

Mercer, J. 1973. *Labelling the mentally retarded.* Berkeley and Los Angeles: University of California Press.

Milon, J. P. 1974. The development of negation in English by second language learner. *TESOL Quarterly* 8: 137–43.

Padilla, A. 1977. Child bilingualism: Insights to issues. In *Chicano Psychology*, ed. J. Martinez, pp. 123–40. New York: Academic Press.

Padilla, A. M., and Liebman, E. 1975. Language acquisition in the bilingual child. *Bilingual Review* 2: 34–35.

Porter, R. 1977. A cross-sectional study of morpheme acquisition in first language learners. *Language Learning* 27: 47–62.

Riegel, K. F. 1968. Some theoretical considerations of bilingual development. *Psychological Bulletin* 70: 647–76.

Rosansky, E. J. 1976. Methods and morphemes in second language acquisition research. *Language Learning* 26: 409–25.

Saville, M. R. 1971. Interference phenomenon in language teaching: Their nature, extent, and significance in the acquisition of standard English. *Elementary English* March: 396–405.

Stockwell, R. P., and Bowen, J. 1965. *The grammatical structures of English and Spanish.* Chicago: University of Chicago Press.

5

Language Switching and Discourse

As indicated in the previous chapter, one particular area of interest within this complex phenomenon of bilingualism has been the interaction of the two languages. One measure of such interaction has taken on the form of switched language use: the use of more than one identifiable language (and the corresponding structures) within the contexts of a second language (and its corresponding structures). This phenomenon has typically been identified as codeswitching (Weinreich 1953), which is distinct from language "borrowing." Borrowing is language mixing at the lexical level with lexicon borrowed from one language. As an example, take the use of *rocket:* "Allá vemos al *rocket.*" Here the term *rocket* is borrowed from English because a Spanish translation is nonexistent.

Language switching is a speech act that multilinguals reportedly engage in readily. Moreover, language users themselves know little about the how, when, where, and why of this phenomenon. Sociolinguists, psychologists, and other investigators are emphasizing that languages in contact reflect intricate and complex sociocultural situations where bilinguals command the ability to utilize two or more distinct language systems.

Research on bilingualism and more specifically language switching is not a new topic of research interest. This combining of different grammatical forms encoded into one form was identified as speech mixture or random intermingling by Espinosa (1911). Haugen (1956) has referred to this phenomenon as linguistic diffusion, and Weinreich (1953) the inability to hold close to either form being used. Espinosa (1956) identified four different forms of language switching: translation *(escuela alta* for *high school); phonetic adaptation *(lonchi* for *lunch);* native morphological adaptation *(baquiada* for *backing up);* and loans (borrowings) imported intact *(balún* for *balloon).*

Lance (1975) reports that language switching is not entirely random, but rather may be due to the style of the speaker and the social setting. For example, if the social situation is conducive to informal speech behavior, sentences such as the following may be generated: "A mi me gustan los hamburgers." (I like hamburgers.) In this situation, Lance might call "hamburgers" a quasi-technical term since it has no direct equivalent in Spanish, unless one wished to consider the recently adopted term *hamburguesa.* Another example might be, "They went shopping, tú sabes." In this sentence the *"tú sabes"* may be stylistically equivalent to the English "you know." Lance also suggests that language switching is not necessarily due to missing lexical items, since these were found unswitched in the subject's discourse, for example, ". . . lo hice en *slice,* tú sabes, en *rebanadas."* ("I did it sliced, you know, in slices.")

Gumperz and Hernández (1970) also see a very direct traditional similarity between code switching and style switching in adults. One such example might be two Mexican-Americans meeting each other for the first time:

1st Man: It was nice meeting you.
2nd Man: Andale, pues. (OK, swell)
          Nos vemos, ¿eh? (We will see each other again, huh?)

"Andale pues" conveys semantic information between the two men and is called a "stylistic ethnic identity marker." However, Gumperz and Hernández (1970) stress that, "while ethnic identity is important as the underlying theme," the marking by juxtaposition or code alternations are more complex than the

simplified example above due to the essential variable of context.

As Gumperz (1967, p. 8) has so eloquently indicated, code switching plays a very important communicative function in many populations throughout the world. Gumperz and Hernández (1975) have differentiated between situational code switching and conversational code switching. Situational code switching is defined by switched language use across social or physical contexts. Conversational code switching identifies switched language instances within a specific conversation, with physical and social contexts held constant. Evidence for these forms of code switching come primarily from adults, and are summarized by the following statement:

> What seems to be involved is a symbolic process very much like that by which linguistic signs convey semantic information. Code selection, in other words, is meaningful in much the same way lexical choice is meaningful (Gumperz and Hernández 1975: 162).

Therefore, code switching has been identified as a common discourse strategy for bilinguals. In fact, Valdez-Fallis (1978) has provided a detailed summary of sociolinguistic switching patterns commonly found in adult bilinguals. Unfortunately, little information on children's discourse strategy, or code switching, is presently available. One such report studied code switching among first- and second-grade Spanish-English bilinguals during classroom activities. The results indicate that the general rule for language use was often "use English whenever possible" (Schultz 1975: 28). For code switching, results suggested that children switched languages in accordance with the listener's language ability. That is, if a child was directing speech toward another child (or adult), his use of Spanish or English was a function of his perception of the listener's competency in Spanish or English (Schultz 1975: 29). Although systematic, code switching seemed to serve a different function in this classroom than that reported for adult bilinguals. More recent is a report investigating Spanish-English code switching among bilingual kindergarten children. The study attempted to identify both situational and conversational code switching among several "academic" and "nonacademic" settings within a school environment.

These data suggest that only one systematic rule governed code switching: "speak the language the listener knows best"(Genishi 1976, p. 2).

According to Lindholm and Padilla (1977), language switching is purportedly employed when a child lacks the appropriate word in the language being used. Furthermore, the switched word will usually be a noun, for example, "Una vez estaba una bird," ("Once there was a bird") or "Yo tengo un car" ("I have a car"). These authors further suggest that when switching does occur, the structural consistency of the utterance is maintained. More recently, Lindholm and Padilla (1979) report that children who do switch languages appear to do so systematically and with intent as the following elucidates:

> Child: "Know what's wrong with your teeth?"
> Experimenter: "What about my teeth?"
> Child (giggling):   "Es chueco." ("It's crooked.")

In this example, the child's "intent" was to exclude and make fun of the experimenter.

McClure (1977) reported that of five hundred language switches recorded in the speech of three- to fifteen-year-old Mexican-American children, only thirty involved constituents smaller than the sentence. Intrasentential (within utterance) switching was virtually nonexistent. Huerta (1977), on the other hand, reports a propensity of intrasentential language switches in a two- to three-year-old Spanish child acquiring English. She suggests that the bilingual child welds the two languages into one language which utilizes grammatical features of both. In a national study involving three Spanish-speaking ethnic groups (Mexican-Americans, Puerto Ricans, and Cubans) Laosa (1977) found differences in the reported incidences of switching. More switching was reported for Mexican-American school-age children; few incidences of switching were reported for Puerto Rican or Cuban children.

A recent study by García, Maez, and González (1980) collected samples of Spanish and English from Spanish-English bilingual children of California, Arizona, Colorado, New Mexico, Texas, Illinois (Chicago), New York (New York City), and Florida (Miami) for four-, five-, six-, and seven-year-old children. A high incidence of code switching, intrasententially, was noted at age four for all children. By age five, a noticeable decrease occurred in switching, and switching virtually disappeared at age six. Regional differences in switching were also reported: children from Colorado, Arizona, New Mexico, and Texas produced significantly higher incidences of switching than children from other states.

Such findings as discussed above have led González and Maez (1980) to conclude:

(1) Young preschool bilingual children exhibit little codeswitching. This incidence increases at age five then decreases markedly as the child progresses through the school system.
(2) Codeswitching appears to reflect the language situation of the home.
(3) There appear to be regional as well as ethnic differences in the occurrence of codeswitching and the conditions which trigger it.
(4) Ability in both languages may be a prerequisite to codeswitching at later ages.
(5) Situational codeswitching emerges first; conversational codeswitching does not appear until age 6 or 7. (González and Maez 1980, pp. 9–10)

These few studies on language switching in children have provided some insights concerning Spanish-English language switching. However, the conclusions of these studies must be considered tentative, owing to the small sampling of both subjects and language productions studied. Moreover, they are restrained to specific ethnic bilingual population and region.

Bilingual Mother-Child Language Switching: An Empirical Analysis

A difference in form between child code switching and adult code switching is suggested in the above reports. It is very likely that the adult characteristics do not manifest themselves until later periods of bilingual acquisition. Yet, it is likely that parental interaction, at both earlier and later stages of linguistic development, somehow affect this final outcome. The present study has attempted to isolate this phenomenon at early levels of linguistic and social development. Furthermore, it has attempted to do so within the contexts of mother-child interaction. In so doing, it has confined itself to the study of conversational code switching. (In this case the physical and social settings were held constant.)

The study has considered as its main unit of analysis the observation of switched language use. Within this general category, three specific subcategories were identified because of their characteristically different communicative functions.

Instructional   A switch to a second language within any one utterance was used to instruct the listener about a second language or to give an explicit instruction about language use. Actual examples include "En español un *horse* es caballo"; "En inglés es *elephant*"; "Say *verde* in English."

Translation   A switch to a second language within any one utterance was used to translate what came before it in that same utterance. Actual examples include "Brincar, *jump*"; "El vestido de la muchacha, ¿de qué color es? *What color is the girl's dress?*"

Code switch   A switch to a second language within any one utterance which does not fall into the above categories, had instead conversational meaning separate from *Instructional* and *Translation*. Actual examples include "Very good, ¿qué es esto?"; "Good, ¿y este?"; "Mira, what is that?"; "Cuenta todo uno, dos, tres *and all the way*."

It is felt that the above qualitative distinctions would add to the pure quantitative analysis of switched language use. In addition, they might suggest the function of language switching during early child bilingual acquisition.

Subjects   The subjects were twelve Spanish-English, bilingual mother-child pairs. Ages of the children ranged between twenty-eight and thirty-two months at the beginning of the study. Mothers ranged in age from nineteen to thirty-three years. Selection of the bilingual pairs was made on the basis of mothers' responses to a language assessment questionnaire. All mothers responded positively to the following questions: Do you speak Spanish at home? Does your child speak Spanish at home? Do you speak English at home? Does your child speak English at home? All subjects selected for the study were of low socioeconomic status (family income was below federal poverty levels) and were participants in a cooperative bilingual-bicultural preschool program in Salt Lake City, Utah. All parents resided in a neighborhood in which 43 percent of the elementary school population was Spanish surnamed. (Only 12 percent of the total Salt Lake City School district school-age population was Spanish surnamed.)

Setting   All recordings took place at the preschool. An experimental room divided by a partition and containing a one-way window was the setting of the recordings. A concealed recording instrument (TEAC cassette recorder) was used to record all language interactions. A total of nine separate monthly sessions were recorded for each bilingual pair. During the first four months of the study, subjects were given a standardized free-productive stimulus instrument (Educational Testing Service Test: *Circus*, productive test 10C) prior to each session. Briefly, the instrument was a two-dimensional picture of a circus. The circus picture contained several items which could be discussed (e.g., animals, clowns, etc.).

Each language session was ten to fifteen minutes in length. At the beginning of each session the experimenter *(E)* presented the mother with the following set of instructions and then left the experimental room immediately.

> Vamos a darle las próximas instrucciones a tu niño: Vamos a platicar un poco sobre este retrato y también de otras cosas. ¿Me puedes decir lo que ves en el retrato? (The experimenter asks the mother to interact with her child using the picture as a starting point.)

During the last five months of the study another type of stimulus item was present during language sessions. This item was a three-dimensional playhouse with a number of fixed objects (furniture, people, etc.). Instructions given before each session were similar to those indicated previously.

Definition of Language Variables   An utterance was defined as any word (in English or Spanish) or set of words; proper names, vowels, or vowel sounds such as "oh," "mm," or "eh" were not included. An utterance was separated from another utterance by a two-second time interval or by the occurrence of an utterance by a second speaker. These temporal boundaries increased the possibility of switched language utterances and were used to measure more liberally the occurrence of switched language. These definitions are portrayed as diagrams (with examples) below:

The One-Speaker Situation

> Speaker 1:   "What is this?"   (two seconds)
>   "What is there?"

In this situation the speaker has spoken, paused for two seconds, and started another utterance. This is listed as two separate utterances.

> Speaker 1:   "Why?"   (one second)   "What is there?"

In this situation the speaker has paused for less than two seconds. This is scored as only one utterance.

The Two-Speaker Situation

> Speaker 1:   "What is it?"   "What is this?"
> Speaker 2:   *"a car"*

Immediately after Speaker 1 has spoken and paused, Speaker 2 speaks. At the end of Speaker 2's verbalization, Speaker 1 begins another utterance. Speaker 1 is scored for two utterances while Speaker 2 is scored for one utterance.

Parallel Utterance

> Speaker 1:   "What color is this?"
> Speaker 2:   "Look Mom"

Speaker 1 has started an utterance but before there is any pause, Speaker 2 begins (and possibly terminates) an utterance. This is listed as one utterance for Speaker 1 and one for Speaker 2.

Switched language occurrence was defined as alternating from

TABLE 5.1

A description of mother-child speech analyzed presenting total utterances analyzed, mean number of utterances per session (the range of utterances per session), and percentage of Spanish, English, and switched language utterances.

	Total Utt.	$\overline{X}$ Utt. per Session	% Spanish Utt.	% English Utt.	% Switched Utt.
Mothers	4,561	76.20 (28–126)	64.13	35.87	9.31
Children	3,747	62.45 (19–91)	56.11	43.89	1.52

one language to another within a single recorded utterance and was classified into three categories. (See previous definition for the exact category determination.) These distinctions allow an evaluation of switched language functions during these interactions. The last two distinctions (Translation and Instructional) are treated separately since they have not been considered instances of code switching in previous research. However, similar distinctions have been proposed by Lance (1975, p. 183).

Transcription and Reliability   The analysis of language use for mother and child was conducted by two bilingual observers. One observer, T_1, transcribed and analyzed all sessions. Another observer, T_2, also transcribed all these same sessions independently.

Reliability was handled by comparing the language scripts of the two transcribers. Only utterances in both transcriptions which were exact duplications (100 percent agreed upon) were used during analysis. This system resulted in eliminating an average of 11.4 percent (range: 2 to 19 percent) of utterances per session from the analysis.

General Switch Language Utterance Results   Table 5.1 presents a general description of the data collected. Specifically, it presents the total number of utterances undergoing analysis

TABLE 5.2

Percentage of total utterances which were code switch, translation, and instructional for mothers and children.

	Code switch	Translation	Instructional
Mothers	4.80	2.64	1.94
Children	1.32	.20	.00

(switched and nonswitched), the mean number of total utterances per session (along with the session range), and the percent total for Spanish, English, and switched language utterances. Both mothers and children were emitting close to equal amounts of total utterances during interaction sessions (a mean of 76.2 utterances per session for mothers and 62.45 utterances per session for children). The percentage of Spanish utterances was higher for both groups, although the mothers' speech was predominantly in Spanish (64 percent in Spanish, 35 percent in English). Of most interest is the small percentage of switched utterances for mothers (9.31 percent), and an even smaller percentage for children (1.52 percent). Therefore, although children and mothers were using both languages during these sessions, few occurrences of switched language utterances were observed (only 11 percent of the total language output was switched).

Code Switching   Table 5.2 presents specific data related to the separate function of switched language utterances. It presents for mothers and children the percentage of total utterances which were classified as: code switch, translation, and instructional. This table indicates the very rare use of code switching within these conversations for both mothers and children (4.8 percent for mothers and 1.32 percent for children). Table 5.3 presents the percentage of switched language utterances which were code switch, translation, or instructional for both mothers and children. For mothers, 40.5 percent of switched language utterances were instances of code switching while 86.09 percent of children's switched language utterances were code switches.

TABLE 5.3

Percentage of switched utterances which were code switch, translation, and instructional for mothers and children.

	Code switch	Translation	Instructional
Mothers	40.50	28.38	20.90
Children	86.09	12.90	.00

Translation Tables 5.2 and 5.3 present information for the relative use of translations within those utterances analyzed. Table 5.2 indicates very few instances of translation for mothers and children (2.64 percent of all utterances for mothers and .2 percent for children). However, Table 5.3 indicates that translations made up 28.38 percent of switched language utterances for mothers. Therefore, although there were few of these utterances in general, they did make up a substantial percentage of switched language forms for mothers.

Instructional Tables 5.2 and 5.3 present information regarding the relative occurrence of switched language instructional statements relative to the general population of mother-child utterances and relative only to mixed language utterances, respectively. As with translation instances, instructional instances occurred rarely (1.94 percent of total utterances) for mothers but made up a substantial percent of switched language instances (20.9 percent).

Language switching, in general, was very low in relative frequency in mothers' speech and even lower in children's speech. Additionally, half of the switched language instances for mothers were combinations functioning to either translate ("What is this? ¿Qué es esto?") or to instruct the speaker ("Say *verde* in English," or "En español ¿qué es *girl?*"). These two types of switched language instances are conceptually different than those previously investigated under the title of code switching. (Code switching has typically taken on a "choice" characteristic; these two categories of language switching beg the "choice" distinction.)

Although it is difficult to speak to issues regarding the qualitative aspects of mothers' and children's code switched utterances owing to their infrequent rate of occurrence, a few cautious descriptions will be attempted. When code switching did occur, single word replacement was more common. For children, almost all (95 percent) code-switched utterances were of the single-word variety. For both mothers and children switches at the beginning or end of an utterance were most common (76 percent of mothers' code-switched utterances were of this type):

Mothers: (1) "¿No vas ir al *movie?*"
(2) "¿De qué color son sus *pants?*"
(3) "Dime qué son estos, *okay?*"
(4) "*Good,* ¿qué son estos?"
(5) "Dime qué es esto, *first.*"
(6) "*Hello, hello,* ¿cómo estás?"

Children: (1) "Me gusta el *monkey.*"
(2) "Mama, where are the *changos?*"
(3) "*Mira,* monkey."
(4) "It's not *rojo, es papel.*"
(5) "*Vente,* I don't want to do it again."
(6) "Where's the *elefante?*"

The function of translations seems to be very clear in listening to the conversations: the mother was attempting to ensure that her child understood her statement by simply repeating it (or rephrasing it) in the other language. The following are some examples:

(1) "¿Qué es zapato? *What is shoe?*"
(2) "El vestido de la muchacha, ¿de qué color es? *What color is the girl's dress?*"
(3) "Rojo es *red.*"
(4) "What color is it? *¿De qué color es?*"
(5) "Green what? *¿Green qué?*"
(6) "Falda, *skirt,* falda *means skirt.*"
(7) "Camisa, *shirt.*"

Of additional interest was the status of each language. In almost all translation cases, the mother was attempting to clarify the meaning of a Spanish term. This suggests that for these "bilingual" children, Spanish was perceived by mothers as the weaker language. This very much agrees with the relative distribution of separate Spanish and English utterances within the entire sample (Table 5.1). Further support of an English dominance characteristic is gained from typical examples of instructional switched language utterances:

(1) "Say it in Spanish, *payaso, payaso.*"
(2) "En Español, ¿qué es *girl?*"
(3) "En *Spanish,* ¿qué es *elephant?*"
(4) "En *Spanish* niño."
(5) "En Español, ¿qué es *horse?*"
(6) Tell me in Spanish, *se va a caer.*"

Owing to this differential language emphasis, it is likely that language switching in this present situation is significantly different from that in other bilinguals. Although this concern is empirically testable, this finding leads to particular caution concerning the external validity of the present study's results.

It does seem clear that switched language utterances in both mothers and children were not a result of linguistic interference. Children tended to keep the languages quite separate and to mix languages primarily at the lexical level. On the other hand, mothers seem to use language switching as a clarification device or a teaching aide. In this sense, some important social-linguistic meaning of language switching is apparent. Although it may not be surprising that parents serve as their child's instructors, the study seems to suggest their active participation in language "teaching." As for further research, it seems valid to suggest a discourse analysis as the next logical step in the analysis of interactions which produce code switching. This has been our own choice.

Interactional Language Switching: An Empirical Analysis

Interactional language switching occurs when a switch in language is observed from one speaker to the next. The following is an exploratory study which investigated a set of tape-recorded mother-child interactions, in Spanish and English, of participants who came from Spanish-English home environments. Of specific interest are the instructional characteristics of these interactions as they relate to the languages themselves and the extent to which interactional language switching occurs within this discourse. The study follows from previous work cited earlier in this chapter. To summarize, the data suggested that mothers' language mixing was made up of translated and instructional types of switched utterances. The present study focused on the discourse of these mother-child interactions.

With respect to the first empirical determination, where mothers are engaged in a teaching situation related to one of two languages, four separate preinvestigatory considerations strongly suggest an affirmative response.

1. All mothers and children were part of a bilingual-bicultural preschool effort which was voluntary in nature. Therefore, it was clear that mothers were very much interested in their children learning both languages.

2. All mothers served on a cooperative basis as instructors at the preschool. Their duties included both curriculum development and implementation in both Spanish and English. Therefore, although professional guidance was provided, all mothers served as teachers in the school.

3. All recordings were obtained at the preschool. Although these were done individually with each mother-child pair and only general instructions concerning the interactive nature for these sessions were given, it is very likely that the teaching format experienced at the preschool influenced the nature of the recorded mother-child interactions. The influence was most probably in the direction of perceiving this interaction as another teaching situation.

4. Previous detailed linguistic analysis of Spanish interactions combined with a parallel set of English mother-child interactions for these pairs indicated the dominance of English speech for each of the children. This is not to say that children did not "know" or use Spanish, but their recorded English was much further advanced linguistically than their recorded Spanish. (See Chapter 2.)

These preconditions strongly suggested that mothers were involved in an instructional process during these interactions. An empirical evaluation of these interactions with respect to the sequential nature of mother initiation, child reply, and mother evaluation (reply) might confirm this tentative hypothesis.

In performing this evaluation, the Mehan interactional analysis model presently used for analyzing the sequential organization of speech acts within classroom lessons was utilized. This model concentrates on the sequential characteristics of teacher initiations, student responses, and teacher evaluations. It was hypothesized that the interactional sequence would also describe the nature of the investigated bilingual mother-child interactions. Some modification of the model was necessary to accommodate the nature of these data (transcripts only).

The investigation provides one of the few attempts to deal with the interactional nature of bilingual mother-child pairs. It also attempts to analyze these interactions as they relate to unbalanced bilingual situations in early childhood. Recent surveys have indicated that the majority of the estimated two to four million Spanish-English bilingual children in this country are characterized by one language dominance. Therefore, the nature of the present mother-child interaction corpus should be generalizable to a very large segment of the presently recognized bilingual population. Of utmost importance was the intent to explore interaction language switching in each of the two language contexts analyzed.

Subjects Four dyads were selected for this study. The children were informally identified as English-dominant bilinguals, approximately three and a half years old, while the mothers were informally assessed to be fairly equally bilingual (balanced) and ranged in age from twenty-three to twenty-nine years of age. These dyads participated in a bilingual-bicultural, cooperative preschool program which was voluntary in nature. (Described earlier in Chapter 2.)

Setting All mother-child discourse took place in an experimental room located at the preschool in which a concealed audio-recorder recorded all utterances. Two interactions per month (fifteen-minute durations) across a nine-month span were recorded. Prior to each of two monthly sessions, the mothers were instructed to speak only in Spanish for one session and only in

English for the other (each session took place on different days approximately two weeks apart). Thus, an equal number of sessions were recorded in each language context. The mother was given a picture of a circus (ETS Test: *Circus*, Production Test 10C) to serve as stimulus for discussion during these sessions.

Utterances   Briefly, the utterances were reliably transcribed from the cassette recordings by two bilingual observers. An utterance was defined as any word (English or Spanish) or set of words separated from one another by a two-second time interval of silence or by the occurrence of an utterance by a second speaker. This two-second interval of silence was extremely useful when investigating silence as a message form.

Specific Data Source   For this exploratory study, three consecutive months of mother-child interactions were selected (January, February, March, 1976) which were in the middle of the nine months of taped interactions.

Methodology   Initial review of the selected transcripts, coupled with a general understanding of the Mehan interaction analysis system for coding, yielded some necessary modifications to accommodate the nature of these interactions and the type of data available (working from transcripts only). While keeping Mehan's sequential nature of initiation, reply, and evaluation intact, we renamed them to accommodate the dyadic discourse: mother initiations, child replies, and mother replies. The subheadings for each of these three sections were also similarly modified (see Chapter 3 for the Mehan Modified System). The major additions in this modification model were child repetitions and mother repetitions. This change was necessary because initial review of the transcripts revealed many repetitions by both participants (especially in the Spanish transcripts).

After a trial test of the modified model and subsequent refinement of the system, two bilingual investigators independently coded each of the twenty-four transcripts (twelve English and twelve Spanish) and each disagreement was jointly resolved.

As mentioned above, each utterance was defined as any word or set of words separated from one another by a two-second interval. Most often this included many sentences or statements

TABLE 5.4

Mother Elicitations

	Spanish	English
% Product	51.6	32.3
% Choice	1.6	19.7
% Process	6.9	19.3
% Informatives	26.3	23.3
% Directives	13.6	6.2
% Mother Determined	92.9	81.3
% Child Determined	7.1	18.7

in each utterance. For coding, each sentence was coded individually, the two-second interval serving to define the No Reply category whenever the child did not reply to a mother elicitation within this temporal period.

Analysis   For each of the three sections of the interactional sequence (mother initiation, child reply, mother reply), the numbers of these initiations were transformed into percentages (for example, number of coded mother product elicitations over the total number of coded statements in the mother initiation part). This was done for each section of the sequence, and therefore allowed a comparison of Spanish interactions with English interactions.

Mother Elicitations: Spanish versus English (Table 5.4)   In the Spanish discourse mothers used slightly more product elicitations (51.6 percent) than in English (32.3 percent). Product elicitations were defined as elicitation acts to which the respondent was to provide a factual response. A typical example in English is, "What is this?"; in Spanish, "Cómo se llama esto?" (What's this called?). The higher percentage of product elicitations in the Spanish interaction and the nature of the product elicitations strongly suggests the teaching of Spanish pronunciation and/or translation. For example:

> Mother: "¿Qué es eso?"
> Child: "Casa."
> Mother: "Una casa, muy bien."

In this typical example, the mother asks a product-type question and receives a product response ("Casa"). Typically, the mother asks the child to identify something. After an appropriate reply, the mother restates the child's product response.

Choice elicitation percentages revealed major differences. Very few of these were elicited in the Spanish context (1.6 percent) as compared to the English context (19.7 percent). Choice elicitations were defined as elicitations in which the speaker provided the response (e.g., "Is it blue or green?"). Process elicitations are defined as acts which asked the respondent for opinions and interpretations (e.g., "What's he doing?"). In the English context, 19.3 percent of the total number of mother elicitations were of this process type while only 6.9 percent occurred in the Spanish context. This finding seems to suggest that the mother is guided to some extent by her previous knowledge that the child is linguistically incapable of grammatically stringing words in the Spanish language (necessary for replying to process questions).

Child Replies: Spanish versus English (Table 5.5)   Major differences occurred in three areas: choice response, process response, and repetitions. There were no choice responses in the Spanish interactions while in the English 18.3 percent were coded. This could be expected since in the Spanish context the mother asked very few choice questions (1.6 percent). The few process responses in the Spanish interactions (9.1 percent) as compared to the English interactions (28.5 percent) can also be accounted for by the few process elicitations by the mother. The majority of child replies in the Spanish context were in the form of repetitions (42.3 percent), while in the English only 4.1 percent of the child replies were repetitions.

Child bids (or child initiations) were similar in occurrence, with 18.6 percent in Spanish and 15.7 percent in English: these bids were coded as successful or unsuccessful in gaining attention or initiating a new topic. In the English interactions, the great majority were successful child initiations while slightly

TABLE 5.5

Child Reply

	Spanish	English
% Product	22.4	27.1
% Choice	.0	18.3
% Process	9.1	28.5
% Repetition	42.3	4.1
% No Reply	16.7	4.1
% Don't Understand	.7	1.6
% Irrelevant Reply	.2	.6
% Bid	18.6	15.7
Successful	4.0	12.7
Unsuccessful	4.6	3.0

TABLE 5.6

Mother Reply

	Spanish	English
% Repetition	39.3	24.2
% Evaluation	33.9	27.9
Positive	18.3	22.6
Negative	15.6	5.3
% Prompt	26.8	47.9

more than half of the Spanish context bids were unsuccessful. Bids were coded successful if the mother accepted the child initiations, and they became the topic for further discourse. This is how we measured child-determined and mother-determined elicitations.

Mother Replies: Spanish versus English (Table 5.6)   The majority of all mother replies in the Spanish interactions were in the form of repetitions (39.3 percent) as compared to the English

(24.2 percent). Again, this seems to reflect the mother's reinforcement of the child's Spanish pronunciation. While evaluations were relatively similar in occurrence, the type of evaluation (positive or negative) differed in both contexts. In the Spanish context, positive and negative evaluations were somewhat evenly distributed; in the English context positive evaluations were relatively more frequent.

Prompting was defined as statements in response to incorrect, incomplete, or misunderstood replies (for example, "There are *Three!*"). The majority of all mother replies in the English context were prompts (47.9 percent). The nature of these interactions was such that the mother and child were continually building on each other's statements; the mother usually completing or adding where the child left off. The Spanish interaction prompts usually requested correction in pronunciation or requested the child to reply in Spanish (not English).

Interaction Analysis   Using the quantitative measures and qualitative structure of the mother-child interactions, different interactional models for each language interaction were generated. Initially, a general interaction model for both interactions was developed which considered the nature of the interactions with respect to topic lengths:

General Interaction Model

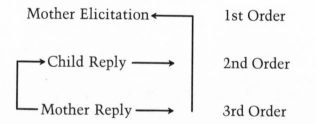

Mother Elicitation   1st Order

Child Reply   2nd Order

Mother Reply   3rd Order

Using the above model, the length of each topic was divided by order for each language interaction (see Table 5.7). A first-order interaction was defined as a mother-initiated topic with the child either ignoring the topic by not replying or by changing the topic by bidding. For example:

TABLE 5.7

Interaction Length

	Spanish	English
% 1st Order	11.6	14.9
% 2nd Order	36.3	53.8
% 3rd Order	36.1	12.7
% 4th Order	16.0	18.6

(1) Mother: "¿En donde están los niños?"
     Child: No reply
(1) Mother: "¿Qué trae puesto la niña? ¿Qué es eso?"

While these orders are not "interactions," they are attempts to start them. Second-order interactions were typified by mother initiation of a topic, child reply, but with no mother reply and followed by a new mother-initiated topic.

(1) Mother "¿Cómo se llama todo esto? Esta es una
              foto, un retrato de mucha gente."
(2) Child: "Azul."
                      End of Topic

(1) Mother: "El está jugando con las pelotas."
(2) Child: "Pelotas."
                      End of Topic

(1) Mother: "¿Eso qué es?"
(2) Child: "Boca."
                      End of Topic

Third-order interactions included three-part sequences:

(1) Mother: "¿De qué color son los elefantes?"
(2) Child: "Verde."
(3) Mother: "Verdes."
                      End of Topic

Fourth-order interactions were made up of four-part sequences:

(1) Mother: "Qué es?"
(2) Child: "Una silla."
(3) Mother: "Silla del dentista."
(4) Child: "Yeah."

For more than fourth-order interactions, (3) and (4) above were repeated.

The interaction lengths for each language were tabulated. For English contexts, a high percentage of the interactions were of the second-order form (53.8 percent). The mother elicited a topic, the child replied, and the mother moved to a new topic. This was also true for Spanish-context interactions. The major differences between language interactions were in the third-order form. The Spanish-context interactions used more third-order interaction sequences. The mothers tended to repeat the child replies (as indicated in the high percentage of mother repetition replies—39.3 percent). Following is a breakdown of the General Interaction Model into Spanish and English by using the interaction length data (first, second, third, or fourth order) and the qualitative nature of the interaction components (elicitations and replies).

Spanish Interaction Model (Figure 5.1)   In this model, the mother elicits a topic, the child replies, then the mother replies. This sequence is followed by a new mother elicitation (new topic). Therefore, it is categorized primarily as a third-order form; or the mother elicits, child replies, then mother elicits a new topic (second-order form). The broken line in the illustration is meant to indicate that sometimes (but not often) the child builds onto the mother's reply usually with a new topic (child initiation).

English Interaction Model (Figure 5.1)   This model differs from the Spanish in that the child tends to build on the mother's reply quite often (and usually with a new topic). The mother elicits, child replies, mother replies, child replies, then mother replies, in a cyclical pattern (fourth or more order form); or the mother elicits, child replies, mother replies, then child replies followed by a mother elicitation (fourth-order form). But, as the interaction-length data show, the majority of the topics in this model were of the second-order type. That is, the mother elicited

Figure 5.1. Spanish and English interactional models.

Spanish Interaction Model

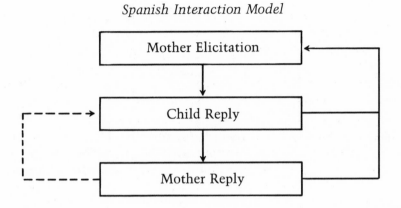

English Interaction Model

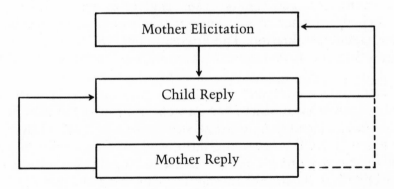

Figure 5.2. Spanish and English qualitative model comparison.

	Spanish	*English*
Mother Elicitations	*Mostly Product* ◄┐	Product ◄┐
	Informatives	Process
	Directives	Choice
	│	Informatives
	▼	▼
Child Reply	*Mostly Repetitions*	Process ──┘
	Product	┌─► Product
	│	Choice
	│	Bids
	▼	▼
Mother Reply	*Mostly Repetitions*	*Mostly Prompts*
	Evaluations—Pos/Neg	Repetitions
	Prompts	Postevaluations

a topic, the child responded, and a new mother elicitation followed. This second-order form is similar to the Spanish interaction but differs qualitatively (see next section). The broken line in this model indicates that the least-used path is that of mother elicitation. This is where the two models differed significantly. This difference seems to indicate that instruction is taking place in the Spanish interaction and not in the English. The Spanish interaction pattern seems to follow closely the classic Mehan sequence of instruction: teacher initiation, student reply, teacher evaluation. The English model might also reflect instruction, but it is doubtful when one analyzes the model in qualitative terms.

The qualitative Spanish interaction model above seems to reveal not only that mothers had a teaching strategy but also that they were aware of inappropriate strategies (as evidenced by the tendency to avoid process elicitations which require linguistically advanced Spanish). While some teaching did seem to have taken place in the English interaction, in general the interaction model is congruent with conversation interaction. (See Figure 5.2 for a comparison of Spanish and English interaction models.) As mentioned previously, 7.1 percent of the mother elicitations were child determined (see Table 5.4). This may be accounted for by the fact that 65.2 percent of all child initiations (child bids) were in the form of language-switched utterances (mostly of the full type—English) and nearly all of these were successful bids. Some examples of this:

1. (Previous Spanish statement by mother)
   Child: "Isn't that his tail there, huh? That's his tail there, huh?"
   Mother: "¿Cómo se dice tail en español? Una cola."
2. (Previous Spanish statement by mother)
   Child: "Look at this."
   Mother: "¿Qué es eso?"
   Child: "Casa."
   Mother: "Una casa, muy bien."
3. (Previous Spanish statement by mother)
   Child: "What does rojo mean?"
   Mother: "Rojo is red."
   Child: "Red."
   Mother: "En inglés es red. En español es rojo."
   Child: "Español."
   Mother: ". . . es rojo."
   Child: "Es rojo."

Child-determined elicitations stem from successful language-switched English child initiations. This seems to account for the broken line path in the Spanish interaction model (see Figure 5.1). And, this same path also coincides with the typical interaction model for the English interactions. The following illustrates this point:

Mother elicitation (Previous topic)
→
Child reply   "What does rojo mean?"
→
Mother reply   "Rojo is red."
→
Child reply   "Red."
→

Mother elicitation   "En inglés es red. En español es rojo."
    ◆
Child reply   "Español . . ."
    ◆
Mother reply   ". . . es rojo."
    ◆
Child reply   "Es rojo."

If you follow the arrows in the above example and apply them to the English Interaction Model and to the Spanish Interaction Model, you can see the cyclical nature of the interaction. At least two interpretations are possible for such a switch. First, it may be that if the child had more knowledge of Spanish and thus was able to produce (respond to) more complex utterances, the models for both interactions might be similar. Secondly, it could be that the child was reverting to English rules for interaction, rules that may have been more familiar and functional.

Qualitatively, negative evaluations and process elicitations seem to have induced child language switches. At least half (twenty-seven of forty-six) of the mother's negative evaluations (Spanish context) were directly followed by language-switched child responses. Example:

(Wrong reply)
(Negative   Mother: "¡No! No te pregunté qué tantos. ¿Qué
evaluation)   están haciendo? What are you doing?
                          ¿Qué están haciendo?"
(Code switch)   Child: "Holding hands."
                 Mother: "Deteniéndose las manos, mijo."
                 Child: "Yeah, manos."

This suggests that negative evaluations led to the child's returning to his dominant language in the quest for the right answer (and positive evaluation). Thirty-six of the total fifty-three mother process elicitations also preceded child code-switched replies. Example:

(Process   Mother: "También."(Glossed Translation: And this?
elicitation)   What's happening here?)
(Code switch)   Child: "He's swinging."
                 Mother: "Está columpiando, columpiando."
                 Child: "Columpiando."

TABLE 5.8

Spanish Interactions: Percentage total and percentage of code switch which involved interactional language switching for mother and child by type.

	% Total	% Code switch
Mother Elicitations		
Product	51.6	5.9
Choice	1.6	8.6
Process	6.9	18.1
Informatives	26.3	19.3
Directives	13.6	10.1
Child Reply		
Product	22.4	43.9
Choice	.0	.0
Process	9.1	85.6
		(14/19)
Repetitions	42.3	11.3
Don't Understand	.7	16.0
		(2/10)
Child Bids	8.6	65.2
Mother Reply		
Repetitions	39.3	16.1
Evaluations	33.9	8.2
		(5/42)
Positive	18.3	2.1
Negative	15.6	23.7
		(4/20)
Prompts	26.8	3.6

This suggests that while the child did understand the question in Spanish, he may not have been linguistically capable (or secure enough) to give a process answer in Spanish. But he did answer! The child's process replies were mostly of the full (English) type of language switching (see Table 5.8).

Language switching by type   For the Spanish-context inter-

TABLE 5.9

Percentage of Spanish Code Switches by Statement Type

Mother—Full	17.5
Mother—Mixed	83.5
Child—Full	72.6
Child—Mixed	28.4

actions, 83.5 percent of all language switching by the mother was of the mixed type. That is, the mother mixed both Spanish and English in a single statement (for example, "Jail, carcel, donde ponen los prisioneros"). In contrast, the child's language-switched utterances were mostly of the full type (English), replying in English when process replies were required (Table 5.9).

The present study has attempted to provide a preliminary analysis of bilingual mother-child discourse. It is important to emphasize that each of the children involved in this study were perceived by both their mothers and their preschool instructional staff as English dominant. Yet, they all resided in bilingual, Spanish-English home environments. Both parents spoke Spanish and English and reportedly (self-report) spoke more Spanish than English to these children. Home interaction data presented elsewhere for these children (Chapter 3) substantiate this self-report information.

The present analysis first centered on the nature of this discourse as it relates to previous investigations of "teaching" discourse (Mehan et al. 1976). What has always been an interesting international question is how parents go about teaching two languages to their children (Leopold 1939, 1947, 1949a, 1949b). Do parents have a strategy for ensuring that their child will be bilingual? A study by Padilla (1974) found that the majority of Spanish-English bilingual parents responding to inquiries of educational objectives wanted their preschool children to speak Spanish. He found that few of the parents themselves had an explicit strategy for implementing bilingualism. Parents relied only on the child's exposure to two languages in the home, and maintained that this was sufficient for their children to become proficient speakers of Spanish and English. This may account for the widely reported notion that children are not balanced bilinguals (equally proficient in both languages). While the mothers in this study exposed their children to both languages at home, they (like many bilingual parents) probably did not insist that their children speak in both languages. In fact, it was not uncommon to observe a parent communicate to his or her child in Spanish and have the child reply in English.

What seems to have surfaced in this study is that there may be an explicit strategy parents use in teaching their children two languages. However, this strategy may have surfaced because the mother was in a school setting, was considered a teacher, and believed in the aims of the bilingual-bicultural program which she helped to develop and implement. That is, the "school" context—status as teacher, planner, and developer of the aims of the school—may have contributed to the explicitness of teaching strategies not present in home environments.

A second concern of this investigation centered on the nature of interactional language switching. That is, what might the nature of language switching in this context tell us of differential discourse strategies? The study of language switching has been generally restricted to an adult-adult interaction model (Weinreich 1953; Gumperz 1967). Results of these adult studies suggest that language switching serves a very important sociolinguistic function in bilingual populations throughout the world (Gumperz and Hernández 1975; Lance 1975). More recent is the investigation of child-child code switching which occurs in many bilingual classrooms (Schultz 1975; Genishi 1976). It is from these studies that the present investigation was launched but with a more direct interest in mother-child discourse analysis.

This analysis indicated that interactional language switching in the present subject population occurred at predictable points of interaction: primarily at those points in which the child's linguistic ability did not match the requirements imposed by the mother. More technically, children tended to switch codes (languages) after process elicitations by the mother. In addition, they tended to switch topics at this same interactional juncture. (In a majority of cases they were successful in changing the topic.) This interactional strategy is not surprising given the less well established linguistic "ability" in the language which the child switches from. It is, in fact, a very predictable strategy that leads to a continued and enriched (process) form of interaction. (That is, more third- and fourth-order interactions.) For these children then, it seems unlikely that they possess a Spanish code, an English code, and a linguistic code that includes the mixing of both Spanish and English. This is in direct opposition to previous studies of adult bilinguals (Lance 1975) and in support of earlier predictions of González (1977).

It seems that the mother-child strategies of this study are adapted to the linguistic abilities and the teaching intent (previously discussed) of the present discourse. Further research in this area should consider these present preliminary findings and expand its search for other "representative" styles of language switching with other populations of bilinguals. This type of research should add significantly to our present limited knowledge of mother-child bilingual discourse.

References

Espinosa, A. M. 1911. *The Spanish languages: New Mexico and Southern Colorado.* Santa Fe, N.M.: New Mexico Printing Co.

Espinosa, A., Jr. 1956. Problemas lexicográficos del español del sudoeste. *Hispania* 40: 31–42.

García, E., Maez, L., and González, G. 1982. The incidence of language switching in Spanish/English bilingual children of the United States. In *The Mexican American child: Language, cognition and social development,* ed. E. García. Tempe, Arizona: Center for Bilingual/Bicultural Education.

Genishi, C. S. 1976. Rules for code switching in young Spanish/English speakers: An exploratory study of language socialization. Ph.D. dissertation, University of California, Berkeley.

González, Gustavo. 1977. Teaching bilingual children bilingual education: Current perspectives. *Linguistics* 14: 53–59.

González, G., and Maez, L. 1980. To switch or not to switch: The role of codeswitching in the elementary bilingual classroom. In *Ethnoperspectives in bilingual education,* ed. R. Padilla, pp. 213–25. Ypsilanti, Mich.: University of Eastern Illinois.

Gumperz, J. J. 1967. On the linguistic markers of a bilingual communication. *The Journal of Social Issues* 23: 48–57.

Gumperz, J., and Hernández, E. 1970. Cognitive aspects of bilingual communication. In *Language use and social change*, ed. H. Whitely, pp. 164–82. London: Oxford University Press.

———. 1975. Cognitive aspects of bilingual communication. In *El lenguaje de los Chicanos*, eds. E. Hernández, et al., pp. 138–53. Arlington, Va.: Center for Applied Linguistics.

Haugen, E. 1956. *Bilingualism in the Americas: A bibliography and research guide*. Mobile, Ala.: University of Alabama Press.

Huerta, A. 1977. The acquisition of bilingualism: A code-switching approach. *Working Papers in Sociolinguistics* 39.

Lance, D. 1975. Spanish-English codeswitching. In *El lenguaje de los Chicanos*, eds. E. Hernández, et al., pp. 138–53. Arlington, Va.: Center for Applied Linguistics.

Laosa, L. M. 1977. Cognitive styles and learning strategies research: Some of the areas in which psychology can contribute to personalized instruction in multicultural education. *Journal of Teacher Education* 38: 26–30.

Leopold, W. F. 1939. *Speech development of a bilingual child: A linguist's record. Vol. I, Vocabulary growth in the first two years.* Evanston, Ill.: Northwestern University Press.

Leopold, W. F. 1947. *Speech development of a bilingual child: A linguist's record. Vol. II, Sound learning in the first two years.* Evanston, Ill.: Northwestern University Press.

———. 1949a. *Speech development of a bilingual child: A linguist's record. Vol. III, Grammars and general problems in the first two years.* Evanston, Ill.: Northwestern University Press.

———. 1949b. *Speech development of a bilingual child: A linguist's record. Vol. IV, Diary from age two.* Evanston, Ill.: Northwestern University Press.

Lindholm, K., and Padilla, A. M. 1977. Language mixing in bilingual children. *Journal of Child Language* 5: 327–35.

———. 1979. Child bilingualism: Report on language mixing, switching and translations. *Linguistics* 24: 23–44.

McClure, E. 1977. Aspects of code-switching in the discourse of bilingual Mexican American children. In *Linguistics and Anthropology*, ed. M. Saville-Troike, pp. 156–85. Washington, D.C.: Georgetown University Press.

Mehan, H., Cazden, C., Coles, L., Fisher, S., and Maroules, N. 1976. *The social organization of classroom lessons.* Center for Human Information Processing Report, Dec. San Diego: University of California.

Padilla, A. M. 1974. Child bilingualism: A study of some Spanish/English bilingual children. Paper presented at XV Congreso Interamericano de Psicologia, Bogota, Colombia.

Shultz, J. 1975. Language use in a bilingual classroom. Unpublished qualifying paper, Harvard Graduate School of Education, 1975.

Valdez-Fallis, G. 1978. Code-switching and the classroom teacher. *Language in Education: Theory and Practice* 4: 13–27.

Weinreich, U. 1953. *Language in Contact.* New York: Linguistic Circle of New York.

6

Intellectual Functioning and
Cognitive Development

Language, Intelligence, and Cognition

Within developmental psychology, there exists an ongoing polemic concerning the influence of cognition on language and language on cognition (almost "chicken and egg" rhetoric). Piaget (1952) has astutely recognized that complex cognitive (symbolic) functioning occurs in young children who have yet to develop only the simplest of linguistic skills. He has proposed that language is but one of a subset of symbolic functioning skills and that language has its roots in early prelinguistic symbolic processes. Worf (1956), on the other hand, proposes that higher levels of cognition originate in linguistic processes. He argues that certain concepts cannot develop until the development of prerequisite linguistic functioning occurs. Vygotsky (1962, 1978) suggests that after the age of two years, emotions, perceptions, and social behavior are intimately related with linguistic experiences.

It seems safest at this time to recognize the interrelationship of language and cognition and hold final judgment on the exact influence of each on the other for future research (DeVilliers and DeVilliers 1978). Yet, this concession forces the consideration of bilingualism as it relates to cognitive development and cognitive functioning. It is these concerns which will be discussed at this time.

Intelligence

After one considers the linguistic and sociolinguistic attributes of early childhood bilingualism, one cannot help but consider the psychological parameters of this phenomenon. Based on information relating childhood bilingualism to decreased performance on standard tests of intelligence, a statement linking the two events is tempting. As Darcy (1953, 1963) indicates, the methodological problems of studies investigating this type of relationship are serious, and any conclusions concerning bilingualism and intellectual functioning (as measured by standardized individual or group intelligence tests) are extremely tentative in nature.

The bilingual population of this country has, both historically and currently, been involved in an enduring psychometric dilemma (García 1972). The use of intelligence tests with the Spanish-speaking (bilingual) children has generated much interest in the differences found between their population and normative groups (Sanchez 1932). Careful examination of the testing literature has revealed several problems that are basic to this area of research. The problems focus on personal, social, and cultural differences. Furthermore, psychometrics has failed to assess adequately the "intelligence" of this bilingual target population owing to language problems (inappropriate linguistic understanding), inappropriate test content, and failure to include this group in the normative sample (Sanchez 1932, 1934; Darcy 1953, 1963; García, 1972; Mercer 1972; Senna 1973; Cleary et al. 1975). The following background information will specifically examine psychometrics in relation to the Spanish-speaking, examining the instruments used and the results of these studies. (It should be noted that in the studies presented here, researchers use different labels to identify Spanish- and English-speaking subjects.)

As early as 1924, Sheldon compared the intelligence of 100 "white" and 100 "Mexican" children of the same age and same school environment. The Cole-Vincent group test was administered and was followed by the Stanford-Benet individual test. Sheldon's results are enumerated in the following four points:

1. The average Mexican child was below normal development of the white child by fourteen months.

2. On a group comparison, the Mexican children had approximately 85 percent of the scored intelligence of their white counterparts.

3. By combining several studies, Sheldon found Mexican children scored lower than American, English, Hebrew, and Chinese children, but scored higher than Indian, Slavic, Italian, and Negro children.

4. As chronological age increased, differences in mental age became greater. A conclusion reached by Sheldon was that the average mental age of the Mexican group seemed to have reached its maximum at nine years. He cited no references.

In 1932, Manuel and Hughes administered the Goodenough Intelligence Test to 440 Mexican and 396 non-Mexican children from the San Antonio public schools. The Mexican children scored in the retarded range based on an age and grade comparison. Garth, Elson, and Morton (1936) tested 445 Mexican children ages eight to sixteen on the Pintner Non-Language Intelligence Test and the Otis Classification Test. This research was directed toward obtaining a reliable, nonverbal test, ascertaining the influence of language and education when subjects' ability on a nonverbal intelligence test was known, and determining how these subjects would perform when administered a verbal achievement test. Results showed these subject to be "inferior" to American whites in verbal tests across age and grade. On the nonverbal test, the Mexicans' I.Q. scores were about equal to the American white children's. The authors suggest that the verbal test could be unfair to the Mexican subjects.

Altus, in the 1940s, reported research findings related to racial and bilingual group differences within U.S. Army populations. An initial study (Altus 1945) examined racial and bilingual group differences in predicting trainees' classification (discharged as inept or kept in the army) and in mean aptitude test scores by using the Wechsler Mental Ability Scale (WMAS) to test American Indians, Mexicans, Filipinos, Chinese bilinguals, whites, and Negros. Resulting scores showed the four different bilingual groups had lower scores on all WMAS subtests than the two monolingual groups. A subsequent study (Altus 1948) addressed the topic of group differences in intelligence and the type of test administered. The subject populations used were Anglos, Negros, Mexicans, and Italians, who had been classified as illiterate when entering the army. The Wechsler Mental Ability Scale B, Form B subtests (information, arithmetic, comprehension, and similarities), the Army General Classification Test (AGCT), and the Mechanical Aptitude Test (MAT) were administered. Results from these comparisons showed that in the verbal subtest, the Anglo and Negro had higher scores than the Mexican and Indian. AGCT scores found the Anglo to have higher mean scores; the Mexican, Negro, and Indian, respectively, followed. MAT scores also found the Anglo with higher means. The other groups were ordered: Mexican, Negro, and then Indian. These data suggested that group inferiority or superiority was in part a consequence of the test used. With this information, previous research examining group differences was subject to question.

In 1953, Darcy reviewed the research on the effect of bilingualism upon the measurement of intelligence. Darcy categorized the research into the following headings: favorable effects, unfavorable effects, and no effect upon the measurement of intelligence. Results of her review found favorable results to be reported rarely. Darcy critically noted the lack of adequate research methodology, since many studies failed to control confounding variables (e.g., socioeconomic status, degree of bilingualism, etc.) in this type of research. However, the research, in general, found bilinguals encountered a language problem when tested with verbal tests of intelligence. On nonverbal tests of intelligence, little, if any, difference was reported. In a follow-up review of the literature on bilingualism and the measurement of intelligence, Darcy (1963) concluded that research attempts should employ research designs capable of handling the influence of variables which had previously not been considered and had led to uninterpretable experimental confounds. Darcy again noted some of these problems in the research reviewed and specifically identified some of the important factors related to measuring intelligence and bilingualism, for example, socioeconomic and cultural background, verbal and nonverbal intelligence tests.

Following a within group strategy, Fitch (1966) compared bilingual first and second graders to fifth and sixth graders on the English WISC. First and second graders produced greater differences between the verbal and performance scores than the fifth and sixth graders: the first and second graders' verbal 78 and performance 98; the fifth and sixth graders' verbal 84 and performance 92. Thus, the difference between verbal and performance scores seemed to be a function of age since only in the vocabulary subtest was a significant difference indicated between the younger and older groups with that difference favoring the sixth graders.

Christiansen and Livermore (1970) compared the effects of social class and ethnic origin on WISC scores. Ninety-two Anglo-American and ninety-two Spanish-Americans between the ages of thirteen and fourteen were tested. The group was divided into middle- and lower-class status. The results indicated that social class was a more important factor than ethnic origin in differences between children. Based on the WISC measures, the lower-class children had significantly lower scores than the middle-class children. In a closer analysis of the results, Christiansen and Livermore (1970) found Spanish-Americans to have lower scores on combinations of the WISC subtest measuring general intelligence, retention of verbal knowledge, and subjects' ability to use verbal skills in new settings. Considering the preceding findings, the authors suggested that in view of the "bilingual nature" of the Spanish-American home background, it was difficult for these children to acquire the verbal skills needed in the Anglo culture.

Killian (1971) studied eighty-four subjects composed of Anglo-American monolinguals (English), Spanish-American monolinguals (Spanish), and Spanish-American bilingual subjects (English and Spanish). A battery of tests was used to compare the groups; the WISC, Illinois Test of Psycholinguistic Abilities (ITPA), and Bender Visual-Motor Gestalt Test (BMVG). On the full scale and performance scale, the bilingual group (mean I.Q. 88 and 90) was significantly different (lower) than the two monolingual groups (English: mean I.Q. 98 and 97; Spanish: mean I.Q. 92 and 93). On the verbal scale, the Anglo-American mean scores (mean I.Q. 100) were significantly higher than both Spanish-American language groups (monolingual mean I.Q. 92, and bilingual mean I.Q. 88). Bilingualism did not significantly influence the difference in performance between the two Spanish-American groups.

A more recent publication by Zimmerman and Woo-San (1972) comprehensively reviewed the research with the WISC from 1960 to 1970. Results generally indicated that bilingual subjects obtained low verbal scores as opposed to performance scores. Furthermore, other culturally different groups (that is, blacks, Spanish-speaking, etc.) generally received below average WISC scores than the standardization population.

The preceding studies described the results of intelligence tests with the Spanish-speaking population. However, most of the studies have utilized English monolingual compared to Spanish-speaking bilinguals on tests administered in English. There has been limited research by investigators administering intelligence tests in two different languages to bilingual subjects. The following studies exemplify how researchers have used language as an independent variable in this area.

The use of Spanish in intelligence tests has varied across studies to include the use of Spanish in only the test instructions, in the entire test, and by mixing English and Spanish. Keston and Jimenez (1954) tested fifty Spanish-English bilinguals by administering the English and Spanish version of the Stanford-Benet Intelligence Test in order to determine the most accurate I.Q. test measure for these subjects. The subjects came from the fourth grade in five schools in Albuquerque, New Mexico. Results showed that scores on the English version were significantly higher than scores on the Spanish version. Some of the conclusions drawn from the data included were that (1) the English version should be used; (2) bilingual children perform better in the formal language of instruction; (3) the use of the Spanish language ceased when these children started their education; (4) variability in range of scores was greater in English than in Spanish; (5) the Spanish test translation was not an accurate measure (translation was done by a Spanish professor in Spain); and (6) the English form presents a language problem. Scores for the two groups were, in the English version, mean I.Q. 86, and in the Spanish version, mean I.Q. 72.

Holland (1960) investigated the effects of bilingualism on the WISC with thirty-six Spanish-speaking children who had been referred for testing. Holland first presented the test question in English and if the subject did not understand or only partially understood the question, it was then presented in Spanish. The subjects were from the first through fifth grades. Holland's results indicated the language problem was greater with the first graders and decreased with added schooling, but was still present in the fifth graders. Galvan (1967) tested bilingual and "culturally deprived" Mexican-Americans from the third, fourth, and fifth grades. Administering the WISC in Spanish and English, Galvan found that the Spanish WISC primarily facilitated performances on the verbal scale. In an effort to consider the equality of languages, Galvan reported correlations with the California Achievement Test to be .46 with the Spanish WISC and .52 with the English WISC. Correlations between the two languages on the verbal scale was .97.

Chandler and Plakos (1969) studied a class of educable mentally retarded students, who could have been erroneously placed there because of the use of an English WISC test. The researchers used the Spanish version of the WISC, *Escala de Intelligencía Weschler para Niños*, developed in Puerto Rico. However, parts of the context were changed to better accommodate the Mexican-Americans being tested. Subjects increased their score by 12.45 points above the English score when administered the modified Spanish version of the WISC. Examples of the changes on the Spanish WISC were as follows: "bolitas de vidrio" changed to "canicas" for the word *marble;* "bola" to "pelota" for the word *ball;* "concreto" to "cemento" for the word *cement;* correct answers were expanded, so the question, "Where is Chile?", included alternatives—"in a can," "in the field," "in the store," and so on.

In summary, several outcomes are suggested by the available data: Spanish-speaking bilinguals scored lower on English intelligence tests than English monolinguals; scores for Spanish-speaking subjects were generally higher on performance scales than on verbal scales of intelligence tests; the use of Spanish in testing the Spanish-speaking remains controversial owing to standard procedure violations and the different scores among different Spanish-speaking populations (geographic); test score difference between verbal and performance categories was greater in the early grades in both languages; social class is highly correlated with test performance; and the need to develop tests relevant to local native cultural norms remains.

A more recent, extensive study reported by Lambert and Tucker (1972) comes closest to answering questions regarding bilingual acquisition and intellectual functioning (as measured by tests). They reported exposing English-speaking Canadian children to a five-year, French-only educational program (grades K–IV). After this exposure, children's measures on standardized tests of intelligence as well as academic achievement were compared to English monolinguals (tested in English) and French monolinguals (tested in French). No significant differences were found between these linguistically different populations. This study was able to control the multitude of variables (socioeconomic group, attitude toward language, quantity and quality of educational experience, etc.) which Darcy (1963) had previously reported as common confounds in earlier studies of this type. It seems appropriate to conclude that bilingualism alone does not lead to any decreased intellectual performance as measured by standardized tests of intelligence. It also seems appropriate to conclude that differences in standardized test measures between bilinguals and monolinguals are not a function of bilingualism but more likely related to the test measures used and possibly to other real psychological differences incidentally co-occurring with the bilingual or monolingual character of the subject population.

Cognitive Development: Linguistic Tasks

In this area we must again begin by considering the earlier mentioned notion of compound-coordinate bilingualism. Weinreich (1953) proposed difference in linguistic processing as a function of the circumstances under which bilinguals acquire the specific symbols and rules of each language. With respect to lexical items (vocabulary), he characterized this relationship in three ways: coordinate pairs would have separate symbols (words) and separate meanings; compound pairs would have separate symbols but only one meaning; subordinate pairs would have separate symbols and share some characteristics of similar meaning (this last category accounts for words which are learned through the translation method). Weinreich was careful to point out that any pairs of symbols for any speaker may be either compound or coordinate and that any pair may move from coordinate to compound or vice versa as a function of that language learner's experience.

As Lopez (1977) reported, this trio of theoretically defined relationships was altered by Ervin and Osgood (1954). By concluding that both compound and subordinate pairs in both languages are associated with the same meaning, they subsumed the subordinate classification into the compound. Unfortunately, this logic brought together under one theoretical term (compound bilingualism) both those individuals who learned two languages simultaneously (usually as children) and those who learned a "second" language (usually as adults). Additionally, most research in this area has directly or indirectly promoted each of these categories (for any one individual) as a total system. Jacobovits and Lambert (1961), Kolers (1968), and Lambert and Rawlings (1969) have produced significant results indicating that compound bilinguals differed from coordinate bilinguals on linguistic tasks which called for the processing of mixed language associative networks. Other more recent experiments have revealed similar results (Lopez and Young 1974; Lopez, Hicks, and Young 1974). These results tend to suggest that compound and coordinate bilinguals differ generally in language-processing tasks. This type of system approach would not allow any one individual to vary within these two categories at any one point in time or to move from one category to another across time.

Unfortunately, the compound-coordinate phenomenon may be restricted only to specific linguistic tasks. Recently reported research (Newby 1976) which tested mixed language associative skills using short-term memory techniques found results counter to those previously reported. These types of contradictions suggest that this theoretical conceptualization may be task related.

Owing to the above definitional problems in conjunction with reported empirical results, it still remains appropriate to conclude (as did MacNamara 1967) that the "overall status of the distinction between coordinate and compound bilinguals, and consequently its theoretical importance, is difficult to assess." With respect to early childhood bilingual acquisition, this distinction is even more confused. If one considers that children are processing phonological, morphological, syntactic, and semantic information in both languages and that information may differ in physical and social contexts, the compound-coordinate distinction seems to become psychologically meaningless. It is reasonable to suggest that any child operating in such bilingual environments may be compound, coordinate, or some mixture of the two across contextual (home, school, neighborhood) and linguistic parameters (morphology and syntax).

Nonlinguistic Tasks

With respect to nonlinguistic tasks, a number of theoretical implications have also been generated by the compound-coordinate distinction. For instance, Saville and Troike (1971) suggested that a compound bilingual first formulates his thoughts in one language and then translates these into a second language. Cardenas (1972) suggested that there is less mental interference in the coordinate bilingual than in the compound bilingual. John and Horner (1971), after reviewing the educational literature pertaining to bilinguals, recommended the compound bilingual as the model for bilingual education programs. As Lopez (1977) pointed out, these types of statements based on an empirically weak theoretical formulation have led to a general state of confusion. Unfortunately, the by-product of such confusion has resulted in the implicit conclusion that bilingualism is a cognitive liability.

Yet, recent theoretical and empirical attention has led to a differing viewpoint independent of the compound-coordinate distinction. Leopold (1939), in one of the first investigations of bilingual acquisition with young children, reported a general cognitive plasticity for his young bilingual subject. He suggested that linguistic flexibility (in the form of bilingualism) generalizes to developmental cognitive tasks. Peal and Lambert (1962), in a summarization of their work with French-English bilingual and English monolingual subjects, also contended that the intellectual experience of acquiring two languages had contributed to an advantageous mental flexibility, superiority in concept formation, and a generally diversified set of mental abilities. Padilla (1977) reasoned that bilinguals must be cognitively advanced because they are able to process information in more than one language. Additionally, many bilinguals are capable of receiving information in one language, processing that information, and producing allied information in another language. (I refer here to the ability of a child to understand a problem statement in one language, solve that problem, and produce the answer in a second language.) For example, Keats and Keats (1974) reported a study in which German-English bilinguals, who did not exemplify weight conservation, were trained to conserve in one of the two languages. Results from English and German posttests indicated that the concept was acquired in both languages. This suggests the possible increased flexibility of bilinguals during conceptual acquisition.

Unfortunately, strong empirical support for the above theoretical formulation is scarce. Feldman and Shen (1972), Ianco-Worrall (1972), Carringer (1974), and Cummins and Gulutsan (1974) have begun to provide relevant evidence. Feldman and Shen (1973) report differential responding between Spanish-English bilinguals and English monolinguals in three separate cognitive tasks. The first, an object-constancy task, required subjects to identify an object (a cup) after its shape had been altered (smashed) in their presence. The second, a nonsense-labeling and switched-name task, required subjects to label familiar items with either nonsense words ("wug") or to switch the names of these familiar items (label a cup a "glass" and vice versa). The third, an associative-sentence task, required subjects to use familiar, nonsense, and switched labels (of the second task) in a sentence describing a relation between the labeled items ("the *wug* is on the plate"). Results indicated significantly increased cognitive flexibility for bilinguals. Ianco-Worrall (1972) compared matched bilinguals (Africanos-English) and monolinguals (either Africans or English) on separation of word-sound, word-meaning tasks. Comparison of scores on these tasks indicated that bilinguals concentrated more on the meaning of words than on the sounds. Padilla (1977) reported similar research comparing German-English and French-English bilinguals to English monolinguals on tasks of mathematical ability and verbal analogies. In each of these tasks bilinguals outperformed monolinguals. The implication of these results includes the conceptual notion of heightened semantic flexibility. The bilingual does not seem to be tied to one particular "meaning" for any one symbol but is able to generalize a functional semantic class.

A similar line of reseach (Carringer 1974) examined the relationship of bilingualism to creative thinking. Four subtests of the Torrence Tests of Creative Thinking were administered to Spanish monolinguals. Comparisons indicated that flexibility, verbal originality, and figural originality were significantly in favor of the bilinguals. Cummins and Gulutsan (1974) compared sixth-grade children in Canadian French-English bilingual programs and monolingual English programs across several measures of reasoning and divergent thinking. These children were matched for sex, socioeconomic status, and age. Bilinguals scored higher on each measure than did monolinguals.

In an attempt to identify more specifically the relationship between cognition and bilingualism, Cummins (1979) proposed an interactive theoretical proposition: that children who achieve balanced proficiency in two languages are advantaged cognitively in comparison with unilanguage children, and that children who do not achieve balanced proficiency in two languages (but who are immersed in a bilingual environment) are cognitively disadvantaged in comparison to unilingual and balanced, proficient bilinguals. This formulation presents most directly the shift away from a disadvantaged perspective (Darcy 1953, 1963) to an advantaged perspective while at the same time continuing to consider the potential negative influence of bilingualism (unbalanced). This interactionist position attempts to account for the success of Canadian French-immersion bilingual programs for English-speaking children and the failure of English-immersion programs for Spanish-speaking children in the United States.

MacNab (1979) takes issue with this interactionist conceptualization on several grounds. First, the data to support the interactionist position are primarily Canadian. Second, these same data have previously been criticized on subject-selection criteria. As MacNab indicates, it is likely that only high-achieving and highly intelligent children were selected for inclusion into bilingual education groupings. Therefore, cognitive advantages already existed prior to bilingual "instruction" and most likely contributed to the success of bilingual development, not vice versa. Moreover, successful subjects came from either middle- or high-socioeconomic strata where education was a premium and learning a second language was openly rewarded. Learning a second language under such conditions is quite different from one dictated by economic depression as well as social and psychological repression of a minority language and culture. In sum, it is not necessary to account for differences in bilingual (balanced or not) and monolingual cognitive performance on the basis of a cognitive advantaged-disadvantaged conceptualization. Instead, it remains possible that individual differences in intellectual functioning combined with the support or nonsupport of the social context for acquiring linguistic and academic skills are the factors for any specific differences in bilingual and monolingual performance on cognitive measures.

Another interesting example of research in this general area was reported by Lambert and Tucker (1972). This study attempted to assess whether bilinguals were more "flexible" in the special case of language learning. Specifically, they asked, "Can French-English bilinguals recognize and acquire (phonetically) a third language (Russian) more effectively than English monolinguals recognize and learn (phonetically) a second language (Russian)?" Their results indicated no significant advantage on this task for bilinguals. Yet, any advantage (or disadvantage) may very well be dependent on the levels of similarity and difference between the languages. This same conclusion may be appropriate for the above-mentioned studies relating bilingualism to specific cognitive tasks. That is, any cognitive flexibility may be associated with the particular task of interest. Future research should more clearly delineate this formulation.

Cognitive Style and Bilingualism

For the bilingual, Ramírez and Castañeda's work (1974) raised the questions relating differing cultural-linguistic experiences to cognitive style. Cognitive style in a young child refers to particular modes of information processing and conceptual categorization of external events. Cognitive style, more specifically in the context of psychological literature, refers to proposed variation in children's perception, recall, transformation, and utilization of external environmental stimulus events (Davis 1971). Research in this area has been generated by previous theoretical conceptualizations of cognitive-style parameters set forth by Witkin et al. (1962) with respect to field dependence-field independence; Sigel, Jarman, and Hansian (1967) with respect to categorization; and Kagan, Moss, and Sigel (1963) with respect to conceptual tempo. Research on these latter two "style" characterizations, although receiving much treatment in the psychological literature, has been confined primarily to age-generated functional change documentation. The field dependence-field independence literature has more clearly reflected a specific concern for socialization variables including issues related to bilingualism. Moreover, research in this area has been relatively more extensive and has specifically involved Mexican-American and Anglo children as primary subject populations. Therefore, it is this research area with the cognitive styles arena which I have chosen to deal with here in some detail.

Witkin and his colleagues have done the most exhaustive research in the area within the last two decades. This work can be characterized by several important theoretical observations concerning cognitive style (Witkin and Berry 1975):

A. Cognitive development is related to psychological differentiation typically progressing from less to more differentiated. A more differentiated system is characterized by separation of what is identified as belonging to the self from what is identified as external to self.
B. Those individuals whose measured perception considers the "field" or context within which an item is embedded are labeled "field dependent." Conversely, those individuals whose measured perception is only slightly influenced by such a "field" are identified as "field independent." Perception is not restricted to the visual domain but includes both tactile and auditory domains.
C. The above cognitive styles are considered processing tendencies. They are to be considered a bipolar continuum.
D. These cognitive styles, besides determining perceptual processes, are also related to personality development.
E. These cognitive styles are rooted in the social character of child-adult interactions during early periods (0–6 years) of development.

Because Mexican-American children have been consistently found to be more "field-dependent" than Anglo-Americans (Ramírez and Price-Williams 1974; Buriel 1975; Kagan and Zahn 1975; Kagan and Buriel 1977), the salient language differences between these two groups are potentially likely to contribute to the different cognitive style findings. Ramírez and Castañeda (1974) have attempted to establish a strong relationship between socialization practices and cognitive styles in a series of cross-cultural studies utilizing Mexican-American and Anglo children. These series of studies forced a conclusion that little diversity in cognitive style exists intraculturally. In fact, Ramírez and Castañeda (1974) have suggested that educational programming for children match to some degree the children's cognitive style. Although such a suggestion is a reasonable and logical extension of their findings, other researchers (Buriel 1975; Witkin and Berry 1975) have found significant intracultural differences on measures of field dependence-independence. More specifically, Laosa (1978) compared the maternal teaching strategies of Mexican-American mothers who were requested to teach a perceptual task to their own five-year-old children. Mothers who had received more years of formal education used inquiry and praise significantly more often than "culturally matched" mothers with less formal education, who tended to use more modeling as an instructional strategy.

The specific interrelationship of bilingualism and cognitive style has received little empirical attention. Only recently have Duncan and DeAvila (1979) reported a direct investigation of bilingual proficiency and cognitive functioning in Hispanic (Mexican-American, Puerto Rican, and Cuban children) first and third graders. Oral language proficiency was assessed in Spanish and English by the Language Assessment Scales (LAS). Cognitive measures included scores on a test used to identify the cognitive characteristics of field dependence-independence, Children's Embedded Figures Test (CEFT), as well as the Cartoon Conservation Scales (CCS), and the Draw-A-Person (DAP) test. The language proficiency assessment was used to identify five relative language proficiency groups: proficient bilingual, partial bilingual, monolingual, limited bilingual, and late language learner. Results indicated that the proficient bilingual group scored significantly higher on the CCS and DAP than any other group. In addition, children with higher language proficiency measures scored highest on the Embedded Figures Test (CEFT). Such findings suggest two cautious but interesting conclusions related to bilingualism and cognitive functioning: A "threshold level" of bilingual proficiency is required before the relationship between bilingualism and cognitive function occurs. Increased language proficiency in either one or two languages is related to cognitive style. That is, as measured language proficiency increased, measures of "field independence" increased on the CEFT and DAP.

This study is one of the first to report specifically such interrelationships. Besides elucidating the specific character of this relationship, the results bring into question the results of previous studies which have investigated the cognitive style characteristics of bilingual children without considering the issue of proficiency in each language of the bilingual. Future replications and extensions of this work which consider the interactive nature of language and cognition in the bilingual will do much to clarify the ambiguousness which presently persists.

References

Altus, W. 1945. Racial and bilingual group differences in predictability on mean aptitude test scores in an Army Special Training Center. *Psychological Bulletin* 42: 310–20.

———. 1948. A note on group differences in intelligence and the type of test employed. *Journal of Consulting Psychology* 12: 194–96.

Buriel, R. 1975. Cognitive styles among three generations of Mexican American children. *Journal of Cross-Cultural Psychology* 7: 417–29.

Cardenas, D. 1972. Compound and coordinate bilingualism/biculturalism in the Southwest. In *Studies in language and linguistics*, eds. R. W. Ewton and J. Ornstein, pp. 167–83. El Paso: Texas Western Press.

Carringer, D. C. 1974. Creative thinking abilities of Mexican youth: The relationship of bilingualism. *Journal of Cross-Cultural Pschology* 5: 429–504.

Chandler, J., and Plakos, J. 1969. Spanish-speaking pupils classified as educable mentally retarded. *Integrated Education* 7: 28–38.

Christiansen, T., and Livermore, G. 1970. A comparison of Anglo-American and Spanish-American children on the WISC. *Journal of Social Psychology* 81: 9–14.

Cleary, A., Humphreys, L., Kendric, S., and Wesman, A. 1975. Educational uses of tests with disadvantaged students. *American Psychologists* 20: 15–41.

Cummins, J. 1979. Linguistic interdependence and the educational development of bilingual children. *Review of Educational Research* 49: 222–51.

Cummins, J., and Gulutsan, M. 1974. Bilingual education and cognition. *Alberta Journal of Educational Research* 20: 259–69.

Darcy, N. T. 1953. A review of the literature of the effects of bilingualism upon the measurement of intelligence. *Journal of Genetic Psychology* 82: 21–57.

———. 1963. Bilingualism and the measurement of intelligence: Review of a decade of research. *Journal of Genetic Psychology* 103: 259–82.

Davis, A. J. 1971. Cognitive style: Methodological and developmental considerations. *Child Development* 42: 1447–59.

DeVilliers, J., and DeVilliers, P. 1978. *Language acquisition.* Cambridge, Mass.: Harvard University Press.

Duncan, S., and DeAvila, E. 1979. Bilingualism and cognition: Some recent findings. *NABE Journal* 4: 15–50.

Ervin, S. M., and Osgood, C. E. 1954. Second-language learning and bilingualism. *Journal of Abnormal and Social Psychology* 49: 139–46.

Feldman, C., and Shen, M. 1971. Some language-related cognitive advantages of bilingual five-year-olds. *Journal of Genetic Psychology* 118: 235–44.

Fitch, W. 1966. Bilingualism and intelligence in elementary school children. *Journal of Educational Psychology* 14: 281–87.

Galvan, J. 1967. Mexican American children's scores on the Spanish and English WISC. *Journal of Genetic Psychology* 86: 113–19.

García, J. 1972. The I.Q. conspiracy. *Psychology Today,* September, 6: 40–43 and 92–94.

Garth, T., Elson, T., and Morton, M. 1936. The administration of non-language intelligence tests to Mexicans. *Journal of Abnormal and Social Psychology* 31: 53–58.

Holland, W. 1960. Language barrier as an educational problem of Spanish-speaking children. *Exceptional Children* 27: 42–50.

Ianco-Worrall, A. D. 1972. Bilingualism and cognitive development. *Child Development* 43: 1390–1400.

Jacobovits, L. A., and Lambert, W. E. 1961. Semantic satiation among bilinguals. *Journal of Experimental Psychology* 62: 576–82.

John, V. P., and Horner, V. M. 1971. *Early childhood bilingual education.* New York: Modern Language Association of America.

Kagan, S., and Buriel, R. 1977. Field dependence-independence and Mexican-American culture and education. In *Chicano psychology,* ed. J. Martinez, pp. 279–328. New York: Academic Press.

Kagan, S., and Zahn, G. L. 1975. Field dependence and the school achievement gap between Anglo-American and Mexican-American children. *Journal of Educational Psychology* 67: 643–50.

Kagan, J., Moss, H., and Sigel, I. 1963. The psychological significance of styles of conceptualization. In *Basic cognitive processes in children*, eds. J. F. Wright and J. Kagan, pp. 73–112. Monographs of Society for Research in Child Development, vol. 28.

Keats, D. M., and Keats, J. A. 1974. The effect of language on concept acquisition in bilingual children. *Journal of Cross-Cultural Psychology* 5: 80–99.

Keston, M., and Jimenez, C. 1954. A study of the performance on English and Spanish editions of the Stanford-Binet intelligence test by Spanish-American children. *Journal of Genetic Psychology* 85: 263–69.

Killian, L. 1971. WISC, Illinois test of psycholinguistic abilities and Bender Visual-motor Gestalt test performance of Spanish-American kindergarten and first grade school children. *Journal of Consulting and Clinical Psychology* 37: 38–43.

Kolers, P. A. 1968. Bilingualism and information processing. *Scientific American* 218: 78–89.

Lambert, W. C., and Rawlings, C. 1969. Bilingual processing of mixed-language associative networks. *Journal of Verbal Learning and Verbal Behavior* 8: 604–9.

Lambert, W. E., and Tucker, G. R. 1972. *Bilingual education of children: The St. Lambert experiment.* Rowley, Mass.: Newbury House.

Laosa, L. M. 1978. Maternal teaching strategies and field dependent-independent cognitive styles in Chicano families. *Educational Testing Service Research Bulletin* 78: 12.

Leopold, W. F. 1939. *Speech development of a bilingual child: A linguist's record. Vol. I, Vocabulary growth in the first two years.* Evanston, Ill.: Northwestern University Press.

Lopez, M. 1977. Psycholinguistic research and bilingual education. In *Chicano psychology*, ed. J. Martinez, pp. 127–40. New York: Academic Press.

Lopez, M., and Young, R. K. 1974. The linguistic interdependence of bilinguals. *Journal of Experimental Psychology* 102: 981–83.

Lopez, M., Hicks, R. E., and Young, R. K. 1974. Retroactive inhibition in a bilingual A-B, A-B^2 paradigm. *Journal of Experimental Psychology* 103: 85–90.

MacNab, G. 1979. Cognition and bilingualism: A reanalysis of studies. *Linguistics* 17: 231–55.

MacNamara, J. 1967. The effects of instruction in a weaker language. *Journal of Social Issues* 23: 120–34.

Manuel, H., and Hughes, L. 1932. The intelligence and drawing ability of young Mexican children. *Journal of Applied Psychology* 16: 382–87.

Mercer, J. 1972. I.Q.: The lethal label. *Psychology Today* 6: 44.

Newby, R. W. 1976. Effects of bilingual system on release from proactive inhibition. Paper presented at Southwest Psychological Association conference, Albuquerque, New Mexico.

Padilla, A. 1977. Child bilingualism: Insights to issues. In *Chicano psychology*, ed. J. Martinez, pp. 111–26. New York: Academic Press.

Peal, E., and Lambert, W. E. 1962. The relation of bilingualism to intelligence. *Psychological Monographs: General and Applied* 76: 1–23.

Piaget, J. 1952. *The origins of intelligence in children*. Englewood Cliffs, N.J.: Prentice-Hall.

Ramírez III, M., and Castañeda, A. 1974. *Cultural democracy, bicognitive development and education*. New York: Academic Press.

Ramírez III, M., and Price-Williams, D. 1974. Cognitive styles in children: Two Mexican communities. *Interamerican Journal of Psychology* 8: 93–100.

Sánchez, G. I. 1932. Group differences and Spanish-speaking children: A critical review. *Journal of Applied Psychology* 16: 549–58.

———. 1934. The education of bilinguals in a state school system. Ph.D. dissertation, University of California, Berkeley.

Saville, M. R., and Troike, R. C. 1971. *A handbook of bilingual education*. Washington, D.C.: TESOL.

Senna, C. 1973. *The fallacy of I.Q.* New York: Third Press.

Sheldon, W. 1924. The intelligence of Mexican children. *School and Society* 19: 139–42.

Sigel, I., Jarman, P., and Hansian, H. 1967. Styles of categorization and their intellectual and personality correlates in young children. *Human Development* 10: 1–17.

Vygotsky, L. 1962. *Thought and language*. Cambridge, Mass.: MIT Press.

———. 1978. *Mind in society*. Cambridge, Mass.: Harvard University Press.

Weinreich, U. 1953. *Languages in contact*. New York: Linguistic Circle of New York.

Witkin, H. A., Dyk, R., Faterson, H., Goodenough, D., and Karp, S. 1962. *Psychological differentiation*. New York: John Wiley and Sons.

Witkin, H. A., and Berry, J. 1975. Psychological differentiation in cross-cultural perspective. *Journal of Cross-Cultural Psychology* 6: 4–27.

Worf, B. 1956. *Language, thought and reality*. New York: Wiley Publishers.

Zimmerman, I., and Woo-San, J. 1972. Research with the Wechsler Intelligence Scale for Children: 1960–1970. *Psychology in Schools* 9: 232–71.

7

Bilingual Education

Why Bilingual Education?

It has always been my heartfelt notion that any endeavor must,
with deference to the past, develop and expand to insure success
and progress. With the premise in mind, and in an attempt to insure
the continued success of bilingual-multicultural education, school
and community personnel must view cultural and linguistic differences between children as positive attributes on which to
build.   Rosita E. Cota, Chairperson, National Advisory Council
in Bilingual Education (Cota 1975, p. 1)

The Office of Education is proud of its program of bilingual-
bicultural education. It responds to a critical need of many citizens of this country—citizens who are making an important contribution to the culture of the United States. If we continue to
recognize and capitalize on the culture and linguistic diversity of
the diversity of the nation in this way, I foresee a growing impact
of this program on national policy.   T. H. Bell, U.S. Commis-
sioner of Education (Bell 1975).

Bilingual education is . . . a jobs program. It's fought for because
it's a way of giving jobs and recognition and status to Spanish
speakers, who traditionally have been at the lowest end of the

socioeconomic pole. The issue is not the unquestionable importance of ethnicity in individual lives . . . the question is the federal role. Is it a federal responsibility to finance and promote attachment to ethnic languages and culture? Why? . . . Would the result be more harmony or more discord in American society?   Noel Epstein, Washington *Post* staff writer (Epstein 1977a: C1)

Historically, these comments summarize the enthusiasm and controversy that have characterized bilingual education in our public schools. Although clearly not initiated in 1967, a national focus on bilingual education occurred during that year due to the adoption of Title VII (amendment to the 1965 ESE Act) bilingual education legislation. Earlier in that decade, President Lyndon Johnson had declared a "War on Poverty." At the time of intense racial rioting both in the Midwest and West, federal intervention in many educational arenas was proposed and adopted. In this initiative, Title VII legislation provided for the funding of innovative projects which would "demonstrate effective ways of providing for children of limited English-speaking ability, instruction designed to enable them, while using their native language, to achieve competence in the English language" (Amendment to the 1965 ESE Act, 1967). These programs were to deal directly with the educational handicaps of non-English-speaking children by acknowledging language difference as a key determinant of educational liability in U.S. English public school.

Not solely bolstered by federal and state legislation, bilingual education received impetus from adjudication of various educationally related questions in the courts. Notably, the 1974 *Lau et al.* vs. *Nichols et al.* decision mandated public schools that serve numbers of children with limited English-speaking ability to provide equal educational opportunity for them. Although not specifically mandating bilingual education as a remedy, it clearly left this approach as a possibility. School districts wherever linguistic minority children formed even the smallest percentage of school-aged children looked to bilingual education as their Lau remedy.

Following these national movements in the direction of bilingual education, numerous state legislatures (Massachusetts, Illinois, Texas, California, New York, Colorado, Utah, New Mexico, to name a few) and local school districts adopted policy and guideline statements concerning bilingual education for those children for whom instruction in English had proven educationally hazardous (Waggoner 1977). As for most educational initiatives, the influence of bilingual education on the children it has served remains difficult to assess and most often a pawn in political dialogue related to almost all facets of national life. Epstein (1977a), in his overview and critique of bilingual education cited in the introductory comments to this chapter, raises critical questions concerning the educational and political consequences of bilingual education. Although such programs were conceived by many to be the champions of linguistic minority children, such programmatic efforts remain relatively few in number, diverse in form, and questionable in function. What is crystal clear is that bilingual education has been and continues to be one of the major educational initiatives of the last two decades in this country. It has received national attention as evidenced by its social, political, and judicial attention at almost every level of government. Although its educational value is still to be judged, its presence in the educational arena has changed the complexion of that arena significantly in areas of curriculum and instruction personnel. In this sense, bilingualism has clearly made its mark on an important institution of this society.

What Is Bilingual Education?

Specific implementations of educational programming for linguistic minority children have taken various forms, themselves based on various conceptual (theoretical) and pragmatic issues related to formal instruction of language and second language. There do seem to exist two general extreme categories of bilingual education endeavors marked by the existence or nonexistence of two languages within the formal curriculum.

Immersion Programs   These programs are exemplified by the Canadian model, the "St. Lambert experiment," reported by Lambert and Tucker (1972). This programmatic approach involves the exclusive use of the student's second language within the formal educational curriculum. Students are treated as if they were native speakers of the second language. As Lambert and Tucker report, this type of program, in French for native-born English-speakers, was an overall educational success as measured by common academic indices: children acquired both English and French linguistic skills and did not differ from monolingual English (attending English-language schools) or monolingual French (attending French-language schools) on various measures of academic and intellectual functioning. These results are clearly in conflict with the findings of similar "immersion" efforts in this country. For prior to the 1967 bilingual legislation, U.S. educational policy with respect to linguistic minority groups could be described as immersion in nature.

Nonimmersion Programs   These programs consider as important the existence of both the native language and second language (English) within the educational curriculum. Most often, instruction begins in the native language and is shifted over a number of years into the second language. But, it is common to find both languages treated as educationally important, although the specific quantity and quality of bilingual instruction may differ dramatically between these programs.

The variety of nonimmersion bilingual education programs are, of course, unlimited. Yet, several models of such programs will be described here so as to attempt a clearer understanding of such variability (see Fishman and Lovaas 1970; John and Horner 1971; Pacheco 1973, for further detailed descriptions).

Transition-ESL Programs   These programs concentrate on using the native language as a bridge to the total immersion of the non-English-speaker in an eventual total English curriculum. Characteristics of such programs include specific concern for teaching of English language in a formal sense and remedial-compensatory ("catch-up") perspective. Native language speaking aides are extensively used in lieu of bilingual teaching staff. Native language instruction in a formal sense is nonexistent. The overall curriculum does not integrate aspects of ESL program; ESL instruction taught is a separate curricular unit. Financial burden for these programs is borne by federal, state, and local district monies.

Transition-Maintenance   These programs concern themselves with the development of two linguistic systems and are most likely to also consider as important the general "cultural" attributes of the non-English-speaking community. The objectives of the programs may be an eventual total English immersion or the continued development of both languages in future grades. Characteristics of these programs include team teaching, pairing monolingual English and bilingual professional staff, or single bilingual professional classroom staffing. The native language is used extensively in subject content areas. Instruction of "language" (both aspects of the native language and English) are most likely to be integrated into various subject content areas. An extensive effort is made to incorporate relevant "cultural" lessons in the curriculum. These lessons usually take on a multicultural characteristic. Monolingual English children are included in the class make-up and are given instruction in the non-English-speaking children's language. Monolingual English children of the same ethnic group as the non-English children are encouraged to participate in an attempt to "restore" the native language. The program is likely to provoke slight to severe criticism from educational and noneducational community members related to the acceptance of language other than English in the public-schooling process. Financial burden for these programs is borne almost exclusively by federal and state resources, rarely by local district resources.

The heterogeneity of programmatic efforts which exist in bilingual education is also common to other educational curriculum areas such as language arts, mathematics, social studies, and so on. What makes the heterogeneity significantly different is the compounded relevancy of the language(s) of instruction. Such increased diversity is most likely a function of the children themselves (their linguistic abilities), interpretation of federal, state, and local mandates, school-district staffing, availability of resources, and the specific prevailing community attitudes toward these programs. In the United States, it seems appropriate to conclude, in consideration of such determining factors, that Immersion programs are rare while both the Transition-ESL and Transition-Maintenance programs share equal popularity. (Within the public-school sector, I am unaware of any truly bilingual program, K–12, whose clear objective is equal linguistic proficiency in academic areas at the time of graduation.) Therefore, the present definition of bilingual education reflects exactly the ambiguousness that exist in the programs.

Bilingual Education in Early Childhood

It is almost universally accepted that language and social repertoires have their origins in early childhood years. It seems that almost all the basic linguistic skills (phonology, morphology, syntax) of adult language as well as important personal and social attributes (self-concept, social identity, social interaction styles) are acquired during these years. Consequently, one motive for early educational intervention has been the potential removal of barriers related to the development of these important linguistic and social attributes. With respect to early childhood programs for bilinguals, it would be important to recognize the linguistic and cultural character of these children in any such effort.

These programs are of recent (1960–70) vintage. Because of the particular language and cultural differences, bilingual children have been labeled "disadvantaged." A change in educational philosophy can be directly related to bilingual children by the following four major recommendations concerning the "disadvantaged" child made by *The Research and Policy Committee of the Committee for Economic Development* (March 1971) which encouraged the initiation of specific preschool efforts in bilingual education (emphasis is my own):

1. Improved education for the disadvantaged is the best hope for breaking the poverty cycle. *But the schools can be made genuinely effective only if there is a transformation of the environment which conditions the attitudes and learning capacities of children and youths.*
2. *Preschooling is desirable for all children, but it is a necessity for the disadvantaged.*
3. Education must provide children and youths with a sense of community and a comprehension of the world of work.
4. Success in the education of the disadvantaged requires the development of total instructional systems which bring together competent teachers, effective instructional technology, and curriculum materials *that are relevant to the interests and needs of the students.*

Examining the actions of innovative educational programs for Chicano children, a report on program evaluation of day-care centers in the southwestern United States (Interstate Research Associates: Mexican American System, 1972) published the following findings and recommendations:

Findings:
1. Lack of authentic materials developed by members of each ethnic community.
2. Monies to date have been allocated to universities and institutions who in turn obtain their information from the local communities.
3. Nonsharing of materials and studies already produced by organizations who have received government funding. They have been possessive with the above.
4. Limited or no parent involvement. Parent involvement is identified by material work contributions.
5. Programs are constantly being evaluated, reviewed, and monitored by unqualified people who are neither bilingual nor bicultural. Our main objection is that this takes away valuable time from the teacher, administrators, and ultimately robs the child of quality services. In addition, findings of these evaluations are not available to the program.

Recommendations:
1. The establishing of material resource centers.
2. Monies should be allocated to local community based organizations so that needed studies may be carried out by qualified, knowledgeable personnel.
3. Parent involvement be on national, regional, and local levels in all phases of the programs—also including but not limited to evaluation.
4. Strict evaluation controls must be established to regional and local levels with the following stipulations:
   a. Evaluations must be conducted by bilingual and bicultural personnel.
   b. Reports of findings must be made available to regional and local programs, agencies, and interested persons. (Interstate Research Associates, 1974)

Most recent, and in line with many of the above recommendations, the Administration for Children, Youth, and Families of

HHS has initiated a national effort to assist local Headstart centers "implement sound developmental, bilingual-bicultural programs" (Arenas 1978). In doing so, efforts are underway in four areas: curriculum development, staff training, resource network development, and research and evaluation.

Curriculum Development   Four curriculum models, each having as a foundation the principles of child development and the language and cultural needs of Spanish-speaking children, have been developed at Headstart centers in San Antonio, New York City, Detroit, and Watsonville, California. Each model incorporates both English and Spanish and is sufficiently flexible and adaptable for use in multicultural settings.

Although based on the same Headstart guidelines, each model has a distinct approach to education. One program, for example, follows a preacademic approach emphasizing teacher-initiated activities. Two are based on a cognitive-discovery approach, which stresses a balance between teacher-initiated and child-initiated activities, and another is eclectic, combining a variety of approaches.

Staff Training   Currently, four bilingual-bicultural staff-training models are also being developed. Competency-based training as established in the Child Development Associate (CDA) program is integral to all four models. In addition, two models are focusing on training bilingual-bicultural CDA trainers.

In these models, staff members are learning to train other Headstart staff members in developing bilingual-bicultural programs. They are also being trained to assist Headstart and local education agencies that are implementing such programs.

Resource Network   A regional resource network has been established to provide in-service training, access to bilingual-bicultural materials, and assistance in implementing programs. This network is intended to serve as a model that other regions can replicate.

Research   Several projects have recently been funded by ACYF to explore issues related to the development of bilingual-bicultural children and their families. (Arenas 1978).

The above specific bilingual effort is embedded within the overall predominant concerns of early children education. Specifically, these concerns are multidimensional in nature but fall within the following general assumptions: early childhood education is not an extension downward of the "formal," 1–12 experience; early childhood education is concerned with the development of children within and outside of the "formal" preschool experience. As Williams (1978) concluded, bilingual education is a natural extension of the maturing of early childhood education and will hold a prominent position in future years.

Implications of Empirical Research for Bilingual Education

As indicated previously, bilingual education legislation began a nationwide trend of great significance. As with many educational trends, this one has as its impetus social and political forces. It was not a program based on a long history of sound empirical research related to bilingual development and bilingual education. Instead, it was a movement cognizant of a new hope for bilingual populations who had previously been ignored. It was never clear that bilingual education would provide effective educational programming, but it was clear that the "traditional" program was unsuccessful. Some ten to twelve years after this initiative, it seems appropriate, at least briefly, to review this educational endeavor and its relationship to specific and related empirical research which it has directly or indirectly spawned. In doing so, I am cognizant of the investigatory paradox: empirical investigations (research) of applied-educational phenomenon most often generate more "new" questions without providing substantive answers to questions they are meant to address. Research in bilingual education is no exception to this paradox.

General Implications   The most direct educationally relevant question reflects the general intent of bilingual education programs: Does bilingual education benefit those children it serves to a larger degree than "traditional" educational efforts? This question certainly requires an answer, and seeking that answer has produced a relevant body of research literature. Unfortunately, these studies are first to admit that the number of variables influencing the evaluation of bilingual education are formidable. The diversity of the linguistic population, curriculum content, teaching models, program resources, quantity and quality of staffing, and degree of community support makes impossible any single statement concerning the efficacy of bilingual education. This is not to suggest that such evaluative research is unavailable. But, it is enough to caution the acceptability of generalized conclusions concerning the educational effectiveness of bilingual education (or most educational programs in general).

As mentioned in Chapter 6, Lambert and Tucker (1972) provide one of the few extensive evaluation efforts related to a bilingual education effort. Recall that the program evaluated, "the St. Lambert experiment," involved the total immersion of native English-speaking children in an elementary French school. Although the formal educational program did not incorporate English as an area of curricular importance, these children continued to live in home environments almost totally dominated by English-speakers. The evaluation of the program was longitudinal in nature and obtained several measures of the children's progress academically, linguistic, and intellectually, and compared these with those of children participating in monolingual English and French educational programs who were equated across several relevant indices—age, general intelligence, socioeconomic status, and family motivation for academic success.

The effects of the program were overwhelmingly positive. First, very few substantive differences between experimental (bilingual) and control (English and French) groups were reported across the multitude of measures obtained. Some differences were observed during the first one or two years, especially differences between bilinguals and monolingual French groups. But, by the fifth year, no substantive differences in intellectual, academic, or linguistic measures were apparent between groups. A later report by Bruck, Lambert, and Tucker (1974) on these same groups, after seven years, finds the same pattern of positive results.

It seems difficult to argue with these extremely impressive results. Children who began schooling in a foreign language were able to acquire and achieve the same educational objectives in two languages without detrimental effects and within the same temporal period as those children participating in "traditional" monolingual programs. Similar results of programs in Canada have been informally and formally (Barik and Swain 1975) replicated. Thus, this immersion model has been adopted extensively throughout the French- and English-speaking provinces of Canada.

Empirical evaluation of bilingual education efforts in this country is not as clear-cut. Cohen (1974) reports one of the first detailed descriptions and evaluations of bilingual programs which involve Mexican-American children. The analysis concerns two bilingual education programs: The Redwood City Project and the Culver City Project.

Redwood City Project   Redwood City, California is a city with a substantially large population of Mexican-Americans. The bilingual education program was not an immersion model. Classes were made up of both Mexican-American and Anglo children with two languages of instruction, Spanish and English. Several academic and linguistic measures indicated the following: Anglo students were comparable to other Anglo controls in English measures. Anglo students did poorly on all Spanish measures. Mexican-American students did generally as well as Mexican-American controls on English measures. Mexican-American students did better than their controls on Spanish measures. Anglo students generally outscored Mexican-American bilingual and control students on all English measures.

Culver City Project   Culver City is a city within the Los Angeles area. This project attempted to replicate procedurally and functionally the impressive results of the Canadian program discussed earlier. Spanish was introduced as the language of instruction in kindergarten for a group of Anglo, native English-speaking children. At first grade, Mexican-American, Spanish-speaking children were incorporated into the class. Although this project failed to incorporate appropriate control groups, the following results were reported after first grade between the bilingual immersion group and monolingual English controls: There was no significant difference between the two groups on measures of English language development and reading. There was no significant difference between the two groups on measures of quantitative (mathematics) development.

The results of this work are not as clear or at least not as comprehensive as those of Lambert. It especially leaves unanswered crucial questions related to the benefits of bilingual education accrued by linguistic minority children, the main target of bilingual education in this country. A more recent and thorough report concerning the significance of bilingual education was commissioned and presented to the United States Congress. This report attempted to evaluate the specific educational influence of bilingual education programming on linguistic minority children. In effect, it attempted directly to answer the important question posed earlier as it relates to the thousands of bilingual children who have participated in the federally funded efforts of the last ten or twelve years.

The AIR Report   In 1974, the Office of Education, Department of Health, Education, and Welfare contracted with the American Institutes for Research (AIR) to conduct an evaluation study of major proportion related to the federally funded initiatives in bilingual education. This exhaustive report was presented in April of 1977 and sent ripples of praise and criticism throughout the educational community. The study took as its subjects a stratified sample of thirty-eight Spanish-English bilingual education sites which were in their fourth or fifth year of federal funding during the 1975–76 academic year. Second-through sixth-grade classrooms, including children, teachers, teacher-aides, administrators, and parents, were considered as providers of important empirical information in the overall evaluative design. As comparisons, classrooms in the same locale containing students matched, as equally as possible, on ethnic background, linguistic competence and socioeconomic status, were included in a two-group, pretest-posttest design. The final sample consisted of 11,073 students, in 384 classrooms, in 150 schools, in 38 separate sites. Moreover, scores on nationally rated achievement tests were used for academic expectancy comparisons.

This effort produced an abundance of empirical information describing critical features of these federally funded projects. Following is a summary of the findings of this report:

1. Although 75% of the participants in the bilingual education programs included in the study were Hispanic, approximately 60% of these students were judged by their teachers as English dominant.

2. Two-thirds of the bilingual teachers and aides reported themselves to be "native-like" Spanish/English bilinguals. Teacher experience in the program was at a minimum of two years with either a bilingual or regular teacher's credential.

3. The average cost per pupil to the bilingual program was $310 (this was in addition to normal district per-pupil costs).

4. Academic achievement measures indicated:

   a. Average Fall 1975 to Spring 1976 achievement gains in English Language Arts for Title VII Hispanic students were not superior to those of non-Title VII Hispanic students.

   b. Title VII Hispanic students who were judged to be Spanish monolingual by their teachers (for test and questionnaire administration purposes) showed no gains in English Language Arts achievement between pretest and posttest with respect to national norms.

   c. Title VII white non-Hispanic student pretest and posttest means showed that the relative standing of these students on English Language Arts declined slightly between pretest and posttest in four of the five grades included in the study (grades 3, 4, and 5).

   d. Title VII black student pretest and posttest means showed that the relative standing of these students on English Language Arts national norms stayed the same or increased slightly in three of the six grades included in the study (grades 2, 3, and 4).

   e. Title VII Hispanic students in all grades (2 through 6) performed better than non-Title VII Hispanic students with respect to the acquisition of computational skills in mathematics.

   f. Relative to national norms, the achievement gains in computational mathematics of Title VII Hispanic students who were judged to be Spanish monolingual by their teachers were greater than expected for all grades in the study.

   g. White non-Hispanic and black students in Title VII classrooms demonstrated positive gains relative to national norms in computational skills in mathematics.

   h. Posttest Spanish Language Arts achievement did exceed that measured by the pretest for Title VII Hispanic students, but lack of suitable comparison groups of students did not permit these gains to be uniquely associated with participation in a Title VII project.

i. In regard to gains in English reading, English vocabulary, and mathematics, several Title VII and non-Title VII classrooms were found to be producing unusually effective results when compared to the rest of the sample. Thus, while educational procedures found in some Title VII classrooms resulted in such unusual gains, these gains were also found in some non-Title VII classrooms.

j. Several Title VII classrooms had students who, compared to the rest of the sample, made unusual gains in Spanish reading, vocabulary, and reading comprehension.

k. No clear trend related to the relative proportion of Hispanic and non-Hispanic students in the classrooms with unusually effective or unusually ineffective English reading or mathematics performance was evident. The percent of Hispanic students in classrooms unusually effective in English reading and English vocabulary ranged from 44% to 96%. The percent of Hispanic students in the classrooms unusually ineffective in these academic areas ranged from 30% to 100%. Essentially the same findings were evident with regard to mathematics performance and Spanish reading performance. (*Evaluation of the Impact of ESEA Title VII Spanish/English Bilingual Education Program, Volume I*, Feb. 1977, pp. VIII-3–VIII-5.)

Any project of such magnitude, whose efforts to evaluate empirically the effect of a particular educational intervention is clearly in the best interest of the children it serves. The present evaluation, more than any other published evaluation, raises critical questions concerning the effectiveness of bilingual education efforts of the past decade. Unfortunately, it fails to resolve the critical question: Is bilingual education an intervention of benefit to language-minority children? The failure of the evaluation to control for qualitative aspects of bilingual and traditional program efforts is a weakness which precludes clear, decisive answers to this question. Instead, the evaluation poses many more questions than it answers: Were projects administered poorly? To what extent were teachers "qualified" to implement and support program initiatives? How was the diversity of curriculum models so prevalent in bilingual education controlled for? How was the adequacy of curricular implementation controlled in such comparisons? Why so much variability in academic results across the programs studied?

Therefore, although this major evaluation effort has taken a comprehensive and critical look at bilingual education in general, it in no way provides the answers to the specific questions of critical concern. Most disappointing, it failed to assess the influence of bilingual education in early childhood (ages two through six), a crucial time for the acquisition of linguistic and cognitive repertoires so significant in later educational achievement.

To conclude at this time that bilingual education programs do not differ significantly from "traditional" English language education programming in achieving academic objectives for linguistic-minority children would be a gross error. Given the language diversity of this country's children and the important role of language in the education of these children, the crucial question is, "What form of bilingual education will significantly influence the education of the bilingual or potentially bilingual student?" Not until ambiguous teacher, administrative, and curricular variables are sufficiently defined and subjected to analysis will the answer to this question be possible. What seems clear-cut in an evaluation of a decade of bilingual education is that bilingual education is here to stay. Its future is not linked to its comparative evaluation to traditional programming. Instead, evaluations of bilingual programs must identify the specific character of the programs which succeed, acknowledging the diversity of languages, culture, curriculum, personnel, and community support which specifically define any bilingual education effort.

Specific Implications

Teaching-Learning Strategies It is always difficult to extract from a body of research literature specific implications for an applied teaching technology. The character of controlled research environments, the uncharacteristic control of intervening variables, and the starchiness of independent variable intervention often precludes relating generalized findings to "real" classrooms. Yet, within these stodgy environments of controlled experimentation and observation, information potentially relevant to bilingual classrooms had emerged. McLaughlin's (1978) review of such research led him to conclude that many misconceptions are prevalent with respect to second language and bilingual acquisition in early childhood:

1. The young child acquires a language more quickly and easily than an adult because the child is biologically programmed to acquire languages, whereas, the adult is not.
2. The younger the child, the more skilled in acquiring a second language.
3. Second language acquisition is a qualitatively different process than first language acquisition.
4. Interference between first and second language is an inevitable and ubiquitous part of second language acquisition.
5. There is a single method of second language instruction that is most effective with all children.
6. The experience of bilingualism negatively (or positively) affects the child's intellectual development, language skills, educational attainment, emotional adjustment and/or cognitive functioning. (McLaughlin 1978, p. 197–205)

McLaughlin is not admitting total ignorance in concluding that the above propositions are false. Instead, he is following the strategy of any "good" scientist: propositions which are extracted from empirical observation and experimentation are to be handled with extreme caution and doubt. It is possible that some or all of the above propositions are true, but to claim their truth at a time when supportive evidence is unavailable is unwarranted and clearly not in the best interest of future research and the applied technology of education.

Is it possible to answer any bilingual education concerns? With the above note of caution in mind, there are some questions specifically related to bilingual education and bilingual research which deserve discussion.

Will bilingual education efforts in early childhood negatively affect children's linguistic and cognitive development? Given the data discussed extensively in Chapters 3 and 6, it seems clear that exposure to two language systems and subsequent proficiency in these two languages does not retard linguistic or cognitive development. That is, children who were operating at complex levels in Spanish were not "retarded" in English as compared to other "matched" monolingual English-speaking children (Chapter 2). Moreover, bilingual preschool children did not score lower on measures of cognitive development than their "matched" monolingual English peers (Chapter 6). Therefore, a bilingual experience in early childhood alone does not necessarily retard linguistic or cognitive development. Unfortunately, important questions still remain: How are differences in the qualitative nature of the bilingual experience related to linguistic and cognitive development? How are cognitive process variables related to bilingual development?

Do bilingual education efforts in early childhood positively affect linguistic and cognitive development? Although there is evidence for the lack of negative effects of bilingual acquisition on general linguistic development, there is no evidence of advanced linguistic development for bilinguals when compared to "matched" monolinguals. That is, there is no report of bilingual subjects' increased proficiency in either language as compared to native monolingual speakers of either language. Cognitively, there is evidence (Chapter 6) that bilinguals score significantly higher on several cognitive measures than "matched" monolingual peers. These measures tend to be those reflecting the ability to consider properties of the environment in a more "flexible" manner: to construct more general semantic categories than monolingual peers. Critical questions remain, however: Are these advantages related to bilingualism or other (potentially cultural) variables associated with bilingualism? Are these advantages related to proficiency levels of bilingualism? Are these advantages related to the specific languages involved and specific cognitive measures (tasks)?

Should bilingual education efforts in early childhood be immersion, transition, or maintenance? There is very little evidence on which to base even the most cautious answers to this question. Certainly previous immersion efforts have been evaluated positively for elementary school children in French-English schools of Canada. A similar conclusion for Spanish-English elementary school children in the United States is not warranted. Recall that prior to the formal funding of bilingual education at the nation level in 1968, the English immersion program was the model for the education of language minority children in

U.S. public schools. That program has proven disastrous for these children (Carter 1970).

Data from empirical efforts in bilingual and cognitive development shed some light on this question. Dulay and Burt (1972, 1974), based on the low incidence of second language errors related to native language structure, have suggested that "incidental" teaching of second language might prove most beneficial. That is, an immersion or transition effort which allows the child to be exposed to the second language as naturally as possible without formal language instruction is suggested as the most effective strategy for second language acquisition. Alternatively, data presented in Chapter 5 of this volume suggest that a formal maintenance instruction system which reinforces the native language, while at the same time formally teaching a second language, produces learning in the second language without harmful effects to the native language. DeAvila and Duncan (1979) provide evidence (Chapter 6) which indicates cognitive flexibility is an attribute of only the proficient bilingual. Monolinguals and unbalanced bilinguals scored significantly lower on a Piagetian and traditional test of cognitive development than did proficient preschool bilinguals. Therefore, maintenance bilingual efforts may enhance both the acquisition of new language structures and provide advantageous cognitive benefits. Of course, sound evaluation of immersion, transition, and maintenance bilingual programs in early childhood are needed prior to any (even cautious) conclusions concerning the adequacy or relative effectiveness of these strategies.

In conclusion, it remains difficult to speculate on the implications of bilingual research for bilingual education in early childhood. It does seem clear that bilingual experiences need not produce negative effects, and many even produce positive effects. Beyond such general conclusions, more questions than answers have been generated by the research community.

References

American Institutes for Research. 1977. Evaluation of the impact of the ESEA Title VII Spanish/English Education Program. Los Angeles.

Arenas, S. 1978. Bilingual/bicultural programs for preschool children. *Children Today* July/Aug.: 43–48.

Barik, H. C., and Swain, M. 1975. Three-year evaluation of a language scale early grade French immersion program: The Ottawa study. *Language Learning* 25: 1–30.

Bell, T. H. 1975. Letter to the recipients of the report of the National Council on Bilingual Education, Nov. 1.

Bruck, M., Lambert, W. E., and Tucker, G. R. 1974. Bilingual schooling through the elementary grades: The St. Lambert project at grade seven. *Language Learning* 34: 183–204.

Carter, T. 1970. *Mexican Americans in school: A history of educational neglect.* New York: College Entrace Examination Board.

Cohen, A. D. 1974. The Culver City Spanish immersion project: The first two years. *Modern Language Journal* 57, 58: 95–103.

Cota, R. E. 1975. Personal statement of the chairperson. In *Bilingual education: Quality education for all children., Annual report of the National Advisory Council on Bilingual Education.* Washington, D.C.: J. A. Reyer Associates.

DeAvila, E., and Duncan, S. 1979. Bilingualism and cognition: Some recent findings. *NABE Journal* 4: 15–50.

Dulay, H. C., and Burt, M. K. 1972. Goofing: An indication of children's second language learning strategies. *Language Learning* 22: 235–52.

———. 1974. Natural sequence in child second language acquisition. *Language Learning* 24: 37–53.

Epstein, N. 1977a. The bilingual battle. *Washington Post,* June 5, p. C1.

———. 1977b. *Language, ethnicity and the schools: Policy alternative for bilingual-bicultural education.* Washington, D.C.: George Washington University Institute for Educational Leadership.

Fishman, S. A., and Lovaas, S. 1970. Bilingual education in sociolinguistic perspective. *TESOL Quarterly* 4: 215–22.

Interstate Research Associates: Mexican American Systems. 1972. Program evaluation of day-care centers in the Southwestern United States. Denver.

John, V. P., and Horner, V. M. 1971. *Early childhood bilingual education.* New York: Modern Language Association of America.

Lambert, W. E., and Tucker, G. R. 1972. *Bilingual education of children: The St. Lambert experiment.* Rowley, Mass.: Newbury House Publishers, Inc.

McLaughlin, B. 1978. *Second language acquisition in childhood.* Hillsdale, N.J.: Lawrence Erlbaum Associates, Inc.

Pacheco, M. T. 1973. Approaches to bilingualism: Recognition of a multilingual society. In *Pluralism in foreign language education*, ed. D. C. Lange. Skokie, Ill.: National Textbook, Inc.

Research and Policy Committee of the Committee for Economic Development. 1971. Recommendations concerning the education of the disadvantaged child. Washington, D.C.: U.S. Government Printing Office.

Waggoner, D. 1977. *State certification requirements for teachers for bilingual education programs, June 1976*. Washington, D.C.: U.S. Government Printing Office.

Williams, C. R. 1978. Early childhood education in the 1970's: Some reflections on reaching adulthood. *Teachers College Record* 79: 529–38.

8

Research and Conceptual Issues

In the first chapter of this volume, I introduced a definition of bilingualism specifically related to the character of this phenomenon in early childhood. It seems appropriate at this time to readdress that definition in light of the data and discussion which have followed and to address both empirical (research) and conceptual concerns regarding this phenomenon. Recall that a definition of bilingual acquisition in early childhood reflected linguistic, social, and cognitive parameters. An attempt was made to conceptualize this phenomenon as integrative, but with a concern for the separate segments that come together to form that integrative conceptualization.

Research Dimensions: Empirical Considerations

The Linguistic Dimension   Most studies of bilingualism in early childhood have focused largely on the structural character of the acquisition process. Questions generated by such studies have been concerned with the order of acquisition of morphology and syntax features (Leopold 1949a; Carrow 1971; Padilla and

Liebman 1975). From the perspective of the child, the primary task associated with bilingual development has been that of "recognizing" that two languages are "under acquisition." That is, two languages are present in the environment and the critical task is to determine the linguistic attributes of each. Therefore, studies of bilingual development, including the detailed report of such a study in Chapter 2, have concentrated on documenting, structurally, the mastering of linguistic milestones.

Unfortunately, even as linguistic documentations, these studies should be seen as exploratory in nature, possibly as one cornerstone to the understanding of a much more complex and interactive developmental phenomenon. While concentrating on linguistic development, the studies fail to incorporate measures of receptive and expressive domains which are commonly reported as distinct in many bilingual children (García 1977; Padilla 1977). Young children may be able to comprehend complex aspects of two linguistic systems, but may only be able to converse effectively in one of those languages. Although there continues to be a lack of data concerned with the receptive and expressive developmental interface in bilingual populations, differential acquisition is often reported anecdotally. It is common for Mexican-American grandparents to communicate totally in Spanish with their grandchildren and to do so quite effectively even though grandchildren speak only English. Many Mexican-American high school and college students report the ability to understand even the most complex Spanish morphology within Spanish conversations without being able to participate expressively in those conversations.

In line with this differential acquisition picture, a comprehensive model describing the bilingual character of any individual should consider as important both receptive and expressive abilities. Generally, the bilingual linguistic character of an individual considers three alternatives: unbalanced bilingualism— L_1 dominance, unbalanced bilingualism— L_2 dominance, and balanced bilingualism. Figure 8.1 provides a graphic representation of this conceptualization where general abilities in L_1 and L_2 are mapped on each other. Figure 8.2 presents a more comprehensive representation of bilingualism from only a linguistic perspective. It does so by including receptive and expressive domains for each language and identifying phonology, morphol-

Figure 8.1. A general relative proficiency model of bilingualism identifying unbalanced (L₁ dominant and L₂ dominant) and balanced bilingualism.

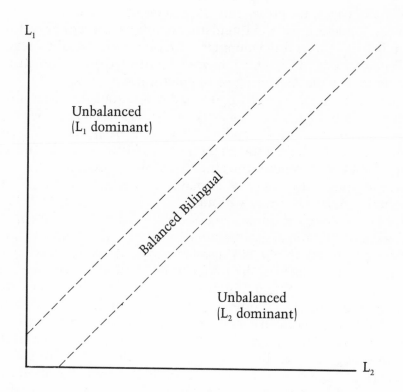

ogy, and syntax as separate linguistic abilities within these domains. Figure 8.3 presents samples of particular bilingual
characterizations as reflected within this comprehensive notion.
Panel A depicts a monolingual L₁ speaker. Panels B and C depict
"unbalanced" bilinguals who can be considered significantly different from the balanced bilingual. Of course, many possibilities
(descriptions) are possible. And, indeed, the expectation is that
these possibilties exist in bilingual populations. Although it is
not clear to what extent each "bilingual type" is represented in
any population, the potential for linguistic variation within any
bilingual population exists. Therefore, even a definition of bilingualism which considers only linguistic characteristics must address the issue of bilingual variability.

Figure 8.2. A comprehensive conceptualization of bilingualism from a linguistic only perspective.

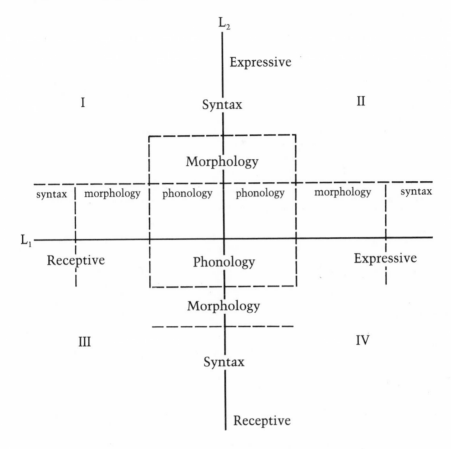

Early studies focusing on bilingualism spawned the semantic concepts of compound and coordinate bilingualism (Weinreich 1953). The independence and/or overlap of semantic fields in young children who are "developing" semantic fields in two languages is an important area still to be addressed. Relying on recent conceptualizations of memory, Lopez (1977), following the lead of Weinreich (1953), has proposed that the semantic system of the bilingual is best conceptualized as overlapping in nature. That is, before any word can be translated from one language to another, it must share a degree of semantic attributes (*rice* shares with *arroz* several similar attributes: it is white be-

Figure 8.3. Examples of monolingual and bilingual linguistic-only descriptions. Each example portrays L_1 receptive and expressive abilities.

A. *Monolingual (L_1)*

B. *Bilingual: Receptive (Balanced)*
   Expressive (Unbalanced)

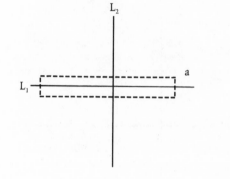

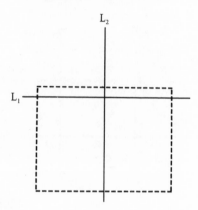

C. *Bilingual: Receptive (Unbalanced)*
   Expressive (Balanced)

D. *Bilingual: Receptive (Balanced)*
   Expressive (Balanced)

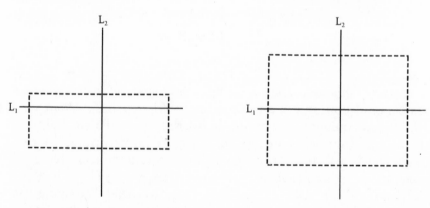

[a]Even monolinguals will be able to discriminate, imitate, and produce some phonology of a second language.

fore being cooked, it is a small grain), but it need not share all attributes (*rice* is bland and is eaten with roast beef and gravy; *arroz* is orangish after cooking and is fried and eaten with frijoles and tortillas). Therefore, the bilingual semantic character of any individual is determined by the extent to which lexical, morphological, and syntactic attributes are shared or not shared in that individual's acquisitional history. If this is the case, to what extent does attribute sharing influence bilingual acquisition either positively or negatively? Does this shared relationship represent a third "$L_1 + L_2$" semantic system significantly different from that of monolinguals? As indicated previously, research in semantic development with emphasis on bilingual children is nonexistent. Yet, this research is destined to be of significance.

The Social Dimension   As previously noted, language is a critical social repertoire. The linguistic component of any social interaction most often determines the general quality of that interaction. In doing so, it carries special importance for the bilingual child where social tasks include language choice. Moreover, like other children who acquire the ability to employ differentially linguistic codes determined by social attributes of the speaking context, bilingual children face the task of multiple code differentiation. Implicit in this discussion is the general notion that languages must not only be mastered in a structural sense, but they must be utilized as a social instrument of value in influencing the bilingual environment within which the child is immersed.

Additionally, it seems apparent that the quality of the social-linguistic interaction has a direct influence in determining the bilingual character of language acquisition. That is, social environments may very well enhance or impede the development of the language or languages of the bilingual child. They may do so by restricting exposure to either language generally or within specified contexts. Also, social contexts may reflect implicit rules related to language use: "In school speak only English." Of course, these may determine more than bilingual development in early childhood. (They may suppress or encourage other forms of social interaction and influence psychological development.)

On a more general level it seems important to recognize the influence of a set of social variables which act directly or indirectly to enhance or impede the development of bilingualism in early childhood. These variables are related to the acceptance of L_2 by the surrounding social milieu. More specifically, bilingualism in early childhood is affected by the character of L_2 speakers in the general social milieu, by their socioeconomic status; political status; absolute and relative population demographics; geographic, employment, educational, religious, and recreational congregation-separation; and immigration-emigration.

Useful accounts of early childhood bilingualism must, therefore, take into consideration more than the linguistic nature of the child's language. They must consider the child's surrounding environment. The environmental context will determine the specific linguistic and metalinguistic information available during development for each language; the specific language use rules for each language, and strategies for code switching; and prestige of the language, and, therefore, the "motivation" to learn-maintain, or ignore-dissipate languages, differentially.

This form of analysis is one of the most needed within the bilingual arena. It is also one that holds much promise in providing information drawn from bilingual acquisition but of direct importance to the understanding of language acquisition in general. For as McNeil (1966) has previously indicated, differential development of specific language features in the course of bilingual acquisition may very well signal important relationships between that differential development and the cognitive (and potentially environmental variables) related to that differential development.

The Cognitive Dimension   Within the developmental area, an ongoing controversy exists over whether language influences cognition, or cognition influences language. Piaget (1952) has long recognized that complex cognitive functioning occurs in young children who have yet to develop only the simplest of linguistic skills. He has proposed that language is a subset of cognitive symbolic functioning. Vygotsky (1962), on the other hand, argues that higher levels of cognition originate in language. He proposed that certain concepts cannot be developed until language has "developed to the capacity" to deal with those concepts. He holds that after the age of two, emotions, perceptions, and social behavior are intimately related with linguistic experience. According to Vygotsky, the child's psychosocial world expands only as his linguistic word grows. At the center of this controversy are the "masses" of developmentalists who concede the potential interrelationship of cognition and language (DeVilliers and DeVilliers, 1978).

For the bilingual child, whose cognitive development parallels the development of two linguistic systems, the interactive potentials are extensively increased. Although only recent studies have considered this interactive phenomenon in young children, previous studies alluded to its critical interaction with bilinguals (Leopold 1939; Peal and Lambert 1962). This interactive relationship has usually emphasized the influence of bilingualism on specific aspects of cognitive domains. Most frequently, bilingualism has been related to the notion of cognitive flexibility— the propensity not to restrict symbolic representation of items and events to specific physically similar instances, but instead to conceptualize any item or event as a member of a large class of systematically related events, differing physically. Moreover, attributes related to cognitive style have been linked to potential cultural attributes including bilingual functioning (Ramírez and Castañeda 1974).

Unfortunately, these investigations have considered only the influence of bilingualism on cognitive functioning. They have ignored the more interesting question related to the interrelationship of cognitive development and bilingual acquisition. In doing so, the implied emphasis of the cognitive-bilingual relationship has taken on the perspective that language influences cognitive development. This emphasis fails to consider an important alternative hypothesis: that the processing of symbolic information and the changes in this processing which occur developmentally, significantly influence bilingual acquisition. It is apparent that the interaction of language and cognition exists. Unfortunately, research on bilingualism has focused on one side of this interaction conceptualization. Even so, it seems apparent that the interrelationship of cognition and bilingual acquisition is important in any thorough representation of the bilingual experience in early childhood.

Interactive Dimension   The linguistic, social, and cognitive

Figure 8.4. A general integrative model of language development.

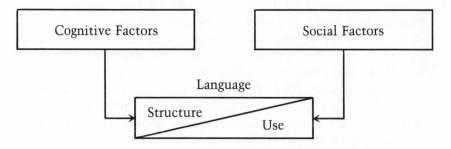

domains of the bilingual experience in early childhood are not only of individual importance, but the interaction of these would seem more clearly to describe the ongoing developmental quality of this phenomenon. Recall that Figure 8.2 attempted to place in perspective only the linguistic character of the bilingual. To this conceptualization, social and cognitive dimensions must be added. Such dimensional additions would suggest the following: the linguistic, cognitive, and social character of the bilingual child are developing simultaneously, and linguistic, cognitive, and social development are interrelated. That is, cognitive processing factors may act to influence linguistic and social development. Linguistic development (the ability to operate within the structural aspects of languages) may act to influence social and potential cognitive functioning. In turn, the development of social competence influences directly the acquisition of linguistic and cognitive repertoires.

This interactive conceptualization is not meant to provide a definite description of the nature of bilingual development in early childhood. Its intent is to reflect the interrelationship between linguistic, social, and cognitive development. Changes in each of these domains may be attributed to changes in other domains, and in turn may further alter the qualitative character of the bilingual. Recent linguistic social (sociolinguistic) and cognitive (psycholinguistic) data related to bilingualism has transformed the phenomenon from a purely linguistic framework into an interactive and developmental conceptualization (see Figure 8.4).

Research Dimensions: Methodological Considerations

Developmental Methods   The methodology of studies concerned with bilingualism in early childhood has most often adopted the form of longitudinal investigation of language development. Children's language is recorded systematically over extended periods of time, or children of different age groups are sampled, usually only once, on certain aspects of their linguistic ability. From such observation, a developmental "picture" is formed emphasizing changes in linguistic ability across time. Of course, these documented changes then serve to generate conceptual or theoretical assertions which will place the specific findings in a more general explanatory context.

Before any extended discussion of the empirical conclusions these studies have produced, and the theoretical implications which they have generated, it is important to assess critically the methodological dimension of this form of research. First, such methodology produces at most a description which hopes to sample representative segments of a continuous flow of behavior. (As in any measure, every attempt is made to minimize the obtrusiveness of that measure.) The product of this methodology allows scrutiny of changes which are observed both within and across specified classes of observed behavior. For language this has usually been morphology and syntax (Brown 1973). Therefore, changes in any specific class of behavior are available for theoretical treatment as the co-occurrence of changes across specific classes. For instance, changes in the obligatory use of the plural morpheme may occur either simultaneously for all allomorphs or only one (Sailor 1972).

Although these analyses allow descriptive statements related to developmental deviation of the same measure, they do not allow experimentally verified cause-effect conclusions. This is not to suggest that longitudinal or cross-sectional data are not helpful in understanding developmental phenomena. But, caution is advised in the generation of explanatory statements from such data.

In the more specific utilization of such descriptive methodology in the study of language, further mitigating methodological constraints exist. Because measures of language are attempts to sample "naturally," these measures typically fail to account for contextual variability. Since language use, especially for the bilingual (see Chapter 6) has been observed to vary systematically, interpretations of changes in language over time which are confounded with contextual variability become difficult to interpret. Moreover, the most extensive longitudinal studies with bilingual children have primarily been reported by parents of such children. Description of actual methods of observation, specific contexts, and systematicity of observation are wanting. This contraint in conjunction with a concern for observer objectivity and, therefore, reliability and validity, decrease significantly the overall confidence of theoretical extrapolation from the data obtained.

With such constraints in mind, it still remains possible to extract cautiously significant information crucial to our understanding of early childhood bilingualism. But, alternative strategies that improve on the developmental methods discussed above are available. A definite improvement would include an extended developmental methodology that incorporates multiple measures of the same class of behavior. For bilinguals, "natural" measures across receptive and expressive domains and varied contextual domains would enhance such descriptions. Parallel measures of cognitive and social measures would further clarify the bilingual experience. These are especially important given the interactive conceptualization of bilingualism in early childhood discussed in the previous section of this chapter.

Specific measures of targetted classes of behavior rather than a "shotgun" measurement would also allow more theoretically relevant conclusions. The previously reported study (Chapter 4) which chose the production of phonemes "at risk" across the Spanish and English dependent variables was able to address the issue of interlanguage transfer specific to contrasting phonological differences in Spanish and English. Although such studies do not allow extended general conclusions concerning a phenomenon, their careful emphasis on only one aspect of the phenomenon will allow more confidence concerning that aspect of the phenomenon. Paradoxically, then, systematically selected extensions of measurement, and reduction in measurement dictated by previous empirical data on prevailing theoretical perspectives can both add significantly to the strength of data obtained using developmental methodologies.

Experimental Methods   An alternative methodological strategy adopted from the psychological laboratory seems also of potential benefit. This experimental methodology requires the manipulation of the specified independent variable while simultaneously observing the effects of manipulation on the specified dependent variables. Such a methodology requires the control of potentially influential variables at the time of independent variable manipulations. In this manner, changes in the dependent variables can be directly related causally to the change in the independent variables. Studies in language and bilingual acquisition have hesitated in using the methodology because it misrepresents the "natural" conditions under which language develops. Yet, in the drive to understand a phenomenon it seems deleterious not to use all the methodological strategies at hand. Each has its advantages and disadvantages. None meets all the requirements of internal and external validity.

In the study of early childhood bilingualism, the experimental methodology seems best suited to the investigation of interlanguage transfer, especially in the analysis of distinct teaching-training practices. The study comparing two methods which differentially emphasized either maintenance or second-language model of instruction, detailed in Chapter 4, exemplifies this experimental strategy. Additionally, the investigation of variables influencing differential use of the languages of the bilingual child are possible by modifying and extending the experimental strategy to nonlaboratory settings. The study described in Chapter 3, in which the introduction of Spanish language "immersion" procedure increased the use of Spanish in freeplay for bilingual children, provides an example of the application of the experimental strategy to the language phenomenon.

Certainly, the implementation of each methodological strategy must be judged specific to internal and external validity criteria: To what extent are the measures employed reliable and the findings representative? At this time, research in early childhood bilingualism suffers extensively on both of these counts, thereby increasing the constraints within which that research can be understood. Therefore, the challenge facing research in this area is not only a quantitative increase in research but a focused qualitative effort as well.

Conceptual Formulations: Bilingual Acquisition

Given the discussion of empirical findings made available in the preceding pages of this volume, some specific conceptual, albeit almost theoretical, remarks concerning bilingual acquisition in early childhood seem in order. Previously an attempt has been made to recognize the potential contribution of cognitive and social factors within a developmental context in shaping the specific bilingual character of the child. In order to generate a more meaningful discussion concerning bilingual acquisition in a theoretical sense, a short review of present theoretical "thinking" regarding native language acquisition will serve as an introduction.

Native Language Acquisition: Theoretical Perspectives   It is possible to conclude that by a very early age, children have mastered a large segment of their linguistic environment. That is, with seemingly little systematic effort on the part of parents, a child has developed a significant portion of linguistic and social interaction competency within the first five to six years of his life. The child is able to understand and produce complex forms of language at this time. Complexity is defined here in terms of the linguistic features discussed earlier: phonology, morphology, syntax, and semantics. In addition, the child is capable of code switches, or shifts, which serve further to clarify his speech productions and his understanding of his social interactions.

How does he tackle this myriad of tasks? Chomsky (1965) considers language as dichotomous in nature consisting of linguistic competence and linguistic performance. The first attribute of language is concerned with the speaker's actual linguistic productions. Chomsky relegates the duties of the child to that of a linguist: the child must determine from relevant linguistic information in his environment the underlying systems of rules in order to generate appropriate linguistic performances. As indicated earlier in the chapter, it does not seem appropriate to restrict our interest in language to a purely structural analysis. Yet, Chomsky's definition served as a theoretical base for much of the research presently available on young children (Menyuk 1971; Slobin 1971; Bloom 1978; DeVilliers and DeVilliers 1978). The structure of children's speech and their ability to perform transformations has been of prime interest. It is true that any analysis of language acquisition must account for the clear performance of children in understanding and producing utterances which they themselves have never heard. As Cazden (1980) has argued, acquisition of language does not seem to be related to environmentally oriented interactions which focus on the mechanisms of modeling or speech correction. This theoretical perspective would hold as most important the genetic base for language development and is representative of a larger nativistic perspective reflected in Chomsky's view of language.

An alternative environmental assistance, "learning" perspective, has concentrated significantly on the mechanism of modeling and environmental feedback in considering the acquisition of language (Miller and Dollard 1941; Skinner 1957; Sherman 1971; Baer 1979). This conceptualization of language has had a significant effect on research which is clinically concerned with language training of language-deviant and deficient populations (García and DeHaven 1974). This research has indicated the effectiveness of training specific instances of morphology and syntax using a training package which includes shaping, fading, and differential reinforcement. Central to these training efforts has been the utilization of imitation of "correct" speech forms and generalized use of trained speech beyond the specific stimulus-response parameters receiving attention during training. For instance, Guess (1969) trained a speech-deficient child first to imitate singular and plural labels, then to label specific singular and plural instances of stimulus arrays without the aid of a model. As training progressed to various singular and plural sets, the subject was able to label correctly never-before-trained plural stimulus arrays. Training on a series of plural arrays produced a generalized plural response class. Similar demonstrations have been made available with young preschool children (García and Batista-Wallace 1977) across various morphemes (Sherman 1971; Whitehurst 1971, 1972).

In contrast to the linguistic and learning conceptualization of language, a more recent third environmental assistance alternative has received research attention. As previously noted, an ongoing controversy exists over whether language influences cognition, or cognition influences language. Piaget (1952) has proposed that language is a subset of cognitive and symbolic functioning. Morehead and Morehead (1974) have directly related

Piaget's cognitive development conceptualization to the process of language acquisition. Vygotsky (1962), on the other hand, argues that higher levels of cognition originate in language. Independent of the locus of control (whether language influences cognition or cognition influences language), there is a growing agreement that the two symbolic processes are intricately related (DeVilliers and De Villiers 1978).

Prutting (1979) has selectively reviewed literature related to this cognitive-language interaction perspective. She organized the development of phonological, morphological, syntactic, and pragmatic communication behaviors in six stages from prelinguistic to the adult level. She argues that the otogeny of linguistic behavior is directly related to the cognitive processes which the child is capable of at various stages of development. Although such a conclusion leaves unresolved the specific causal relationship between cognition and language, it clearly provides a conceptualization of language development cognizant of the relationship. Moreover, much like Piaget (1952), this stage-process position holds that the child is an active participant in his own development. Linguistic development is not seen as singly determined by some genetic codes or selective schedules of reinforcement. Instead, language seems to be determined by the forces of maturation, cognitive development, and the social-linguistic environment.

In sum, native language acquisition must presently be considered within several conceptual domains. It seems most appropriate to acknowledge at least three major theoretical orientations—linguistic, learning, and cognitive. It seems just as appropriate to emphasize that each position possesses its supporters and detractors. But, empirical research generated by each position has clearly advanced our understanding of language acquisition by emphasizing the empirical phenomena and alternative processes which may account for these phenomena. It seems evident that language acquisition is systematic. It can be described as developmental in character, dependent on its past character, and its development significantly related to environmental-social interaction (see Figure 8.4). Although the descriptive account of its developmental character is unfolding, the exact causal relationship between environmental, cognitive, and linguistic parameters continues to be explored from these three "theoretical" perspectives.

Bilingual Acquisition: Theoretical Perspectives   Like native language acquisition, bilingual acquisition is best perceived as a product of both cognitive and social factors. Paradoxically, this phenomenon must be seen as both similar to and different from monolingual development. At the empirical level, the following tentative conclusions concerning bilingualism are supported by evidence gathered on various bilingual populations of young children. (1) Children can and do acquire more than one language during early childhood. (2) The acquisition of two languages need not hamper developmentally the acquisition of either language. (3) The acquisition of two languages can be parallel, but need not be. That is, the qualitative character of one language may lag behind, surge ahead of, or develop simultaneously with the other language. (4) The acquisition of two languages may result in an "interlanguage," incorporating structural aspects of both languages. This need not be the case. That is, languages may develop separately, with "mixed" forms a rarity. (5) Linguistic transfer phenomena have been reported such that specific structures of the dominant language influence the developmental quality of the less-dominant language, or they influence the developmental character of two languages only minimally. (6) Bilingual children have been found to score both higher and lower than monolingual children on specific and general measures of cognitive development, intelligence, and school achievement.

A careful review of the conclusions above indicates that except for the first two conclusions, contradictions concerning the empirical basis for theoretical formulations are the rule, rather than the desired exception. If one disregards the possible methodological incongruencies of the reported research in accounting for such contradictions (and, at the present time this is not a recommended strategy), what theoretical statements are actually possible?

If forced to make any statement regarding these discrepancies in the data, it seems defensible to suggest the overall importance of the social environment in accounting for the specific character of bilingual development. That is, specific discrepancies regarding the parallel versus nonparallel development (3), the separate versus interlanguage development (4), the influence of L_1 versus the noninfluence of L_2 (5), and the cognitive advantaged versus the cognitive disadvantaged (6) character of bilingual development may very well have their origin in the differential bilingual social milieus occupied by children or groups of children during early childhood. The task awaiting empirical researchers following such a theoretical thrust is to isolate these social variables which individually or as a group directly or indirectly influence bilingual acquisition.

Such a strategy would not exclude the more traditional study of the acquisition of linguistic structures. But such studies should extend themselves in such a manner as to include social environments as an independent variable. The studies of cognition and bilingualism should also incorporate potentially significant social milieu variables in addition to structural measures of language and cognition. In so doing, future research will reflect the integrative function of linguistic, social, and cognitive factors in arriving at a comprehensive understanding, theoretically, of bilingual acquisition in early childhood.

Conceptual Formulations: Bilingual Acquisition and Language Acquisition

In the previous section, factors identified as important to bilingual acquisition were shown to be consistently related to conceptual formulations of monolingual, native language acquisition. Clearly, research in bilingual and second language acquisition has borrowed extensively, methodologically and otherwise, from this early work. But, the reverse has also occurred. Recall that Leopold (1939, 1947, 1949a, 1949b) was one of the first major contributors to our present understanding of bilingual acquisition with his intricate and thoughtful presentation of language development data concerning his German- and English-speaking daughter. Yet, Leopold's work also influenced both methodologically and theoretically the later work of developmental psycholinguists (Bloom 1978). Although Leopold's major interest was the description of bilingual development, his attention to developmental changes as well as his emphasis on ordered development of morphology and syntax was to influence newer generations of researchers whose primary interest was native language acquisition.

The study of bilingualism in early childhood should be seen as a significant area of research with much to contribute regarding the understanding of language acquisition in general. The bilingual child offers a set of linguistic, cognitive, and social circumstances which make it one of those sought-after "natural experiments" of nature. McNeil (1966) has suggested that the study of bilingual acquisition may very well offer information regarding linguistic universals not obtainable by individual study of the acquisition of one language or the comparative study of the acquisition of different languages of children who are individual members of independent linguistic societies. Bowerman (1975) and Braine (1976) have reported analysis of this last type. They were interested in the developmental sequence of semantic and syntactic features of native language speakers of English, Finnish, Samoan, Luo, and other western European languages. Such studies are meant to extend and validate conceptualizations of language acquisition which were originally conducted on native English speakers. Moreover, they highlight universal cognitive considerations important in understanding the acquisition of language. The same can be said about the study of bilingual acquisition. For the bilingual, the child serves as its own control. If differences in the acquisition of language (for instance the order of acquisition of syntactic or semantic features) are observed, they cannot be attributed to individual variation. On the other hand, similarities between the development of two languages in the bilingual and that of the monolingual development provide supportive evidence for the possibility of linguistic and cognitive universals.

The study of bilingual acquisition has potential significance for a better understanding of the role of social variables in the acquisition and use of language in general. Bilinguals come in various linguistic "shapes and forms," from equally proficient in both languages to shades of dominance of one language over another. By such manipulations of nature, researchers may be able to identify the social variables to which such a bilingual character may be associated. In doing so, such studies identify variables of potential significance to the development of language in general.

In Chapter 2, bilingual children were found to be "further advanced" in English than Spanish. Yet, home language observations revealed that child-mother speech was made up of both languages, with Spanish interaction predominating. These same home observations, however, also indicated that child-sibling speech was heavily weighted in English, with only a few Spanish interactions observed. For these bilingual children, it was very possible that sibling interaction was clearly more important for language acquisition than parent-child interaction. This, of course, is one of several possible explanations of the resultant unequivalence of Spanish and English development. But, it serves to exemplify the potential value in the study of such bilingual situations in search of significant variables related to language acquisition. Such studies can isolate the natural occurrences of parameters of quality and quantity of exposure to each language, the social acceptability and constraints placed on each language, the social boundaries of each language, and the communicative function of each language, to name only a few.

Of course, the potential relationship between bilingualism and cognition has been discussed (Chapter 6). The causal interface of cognition and language has also been discussed elsewhere (Clark 1974; Morehead and Morehead 1974). The study of early childhood bilingualism will do much to enlighten this general area as well. The young bilingual serves as the best example of complex symbolic processing. This is especially true in those cases where the languages of the bilingual differ significantly, morphologically, and syntactically. To what degree in general is symbolic functioning enhanced? To what degree is symbolic functioning impaired? To what degree are cognitive processes modified by such symbolic-linguistic demands? To what degree is linguistic functioning altered by factors such as symbolic-linguistic demands? No doubt, answers to these questions would enhance greatly our overall understanding of cognitive and linguistic functioning and the independence-interdependence of those processes related to such functioning.

Without question, the study of early childhood bilingualism will provide important empirical, theoretical, and applied information regarding multiple language acquisition. But such research must also be seen as adding to our general understanding of language acquisition and its relationship to cognitive and social factors. Too often bilingual research is seen benefiting only a specific segment of our world society. Instead, it should be evaluated with interest by even those whose special interest lies in native language acquisition. Of course, for bilingual investigations to serve as contributions to the broader area of language development, researchers in this "specialty" area themselves must take the time and initiative to sound the significance of their work to broader audiences of research professionals. Only then will the potential contributions be realized. With such efforts, research in early childhood bilingualism becomes an important field of inquiry for more than a select group of today's children. Instead, systematic inquiry into the bilingual phenomenon will generate a more comprehensive view of one of the most important tasks of any young child: to master the language(s) of those individuals whom he or she joins as a social member.

References

Baer, D. M. 1979. The organism as host. *Human Development* 19: 87–98.

Bloom, L. 1978. *Readings in language development.* New York: John Wiley and Sons.

Bowerman, M. 1975. Crosslinguistic similarities at two stages of syntactic development. In *Foundations of language development. Vol. I,* eds. E. Lenneberg and E. Lenneberg, pp. 267–82. London: UNESCO Press.

Braine, M. D. S. 1976. Children's first word combinations. *Monographs of the Society for Research in Child Development.*

Brown, R. 1973. *A first language: The early stages.* Cambridge, Mass.: Harvard University Press.

Carrow, E. 1971. Comprehension of English and Spanish by preschool Mexican American children. *Modern Language Journal* 55: 299–307.

———. 1972. Auditory comprehension of English by monolingual and bilingual preschool children. *Journal of Speech and Hearing Research* 15: 407–12.

Cazden, C. 1980. Language development and the preschool environment. In *Language in early childhood education,* ed. C. Cazden. Washington, D.C.: NAEYC.

Chomsky, N. 1965. *Aspects of the theory of syntax.* Cambridge, Mass.: MIT Press.

Clark, E. V. 1974. Some aspects of conceptual basis for first language

222 *Chapter 8*

222 *Chapter 8*

222   *Chapter 8*

222 *Chapter 8*

acquisition. In *Language perspectives: acquisition, retardation and intervention*, eds. R. C. Scheifelbusch and L. L. Lloyd, pp. 105–28. Baltimore: University Park Press.

DeVilliers, J., and DeVilliers, P. 1978. *Language acquisition.* Cambridge, Mass.: Harvard University Press.

García, E. 1977. Strategies for bilingual research. In *Chicano psychology*, ed. J. V. Martinez, pp. 141–54. New York: Academic Press.

García, E., and Batista-Wallace, M. 1977. Parental training of the plural morpheme in normal toddlers. *Journal of Applied Behavior Analysis* 10: 96–99.

García, E., and DeHaven, E. 1974. Use of operant techniques in the establishment of generalization of language: A review and analysis. *American Journal of Mental Deficiency* 79: 169–78.

Guess, D. 1969. A functional analysis of receptive language and productive speech: Acquisition of the plural morpheme. *Journal of Applied Behavior Analysis* 4: 101–12.

Leopold, W. F. 1939. *Speech development of a bilingual child: A linguist's record. Vol. I, Vocabulary growth in the first two years.* Evanston, Ill.: Northwestern University Press.

———. 1947. *Speech development of a bilingual child: A linguist's record. Vol. II, Sound learning in the first two years.* Evanston, Ill.: Northwestern University Press.

———. 1949a. *Speech development of a bilingual child: A linguist's record. Vol. III, Grammars and general problems in the first two years.* Evanston, Ill.: Northwestern University Press.

———. 1949b. *Speech development of a bilingual child: A linguist's record. Vol. IV, Diary from age two.* Evanston, Ill.: Northwestern University Press.

Lopez, M. Psycholinguistic research and bilingual education. In *Chicano psychology*, ed. J. Martinez, pp. 127–40. New York: Academic Press.

McNiel, D. 1966. Developmental psycholinguistics. In *The genesis of language: A psycholinguistic approach*, eds. F. Smith and G. Miller, pp. 15–84. Cambridge, Mass.: MIT Press.

Menyuk, P. 1971. *The acquisition and development of language.* Englewood Cliffs, N.J.: Prentice-Hall, Inc.

Miller, N. E., and Dollard, J. 1941. *Social learning and imitation.* New Haven: Yale University Press.

Morehead, D. M., and Morehead, A. M. 1974. From signal to sign: A piagetian view of thought and language during the first two years. In *Language perspectives: acquisition, retardation and intervention*, eds. R. L. Schiefelbusch and L. L. Lloyd, pp. 129–52. Baltimore: University Park Press.

Padilla, A. M., and Liebman, E. 1975. Language acquisition in the bilingual child. *The bilingual review/La revista bilingue* 2: 34–55.

Padilla, A. 1977. Child bilingualism: Insights to issues. In *Chicano psychology*, ed. J. Martinez, pp. 111–26. New York: Academic Press.

Peal, E., and Lambert, W. E. 1962. The relation of bilingualism to intelligence. *Psychological Monographs General and Applied* 76: 1–23.

Piaget, J. 1952. *The origins of intelligence in children*. Englewood Cliffs, N.J.: Prentice-Hall.

Prutting, C. A. 1979. Process /'pras/, ses/n: The action of moving forward progressively from one point to another on the way to completion. *Journal of Speech and Hearing Disorder* 26: 185–98.

Ramírez III, M., and Castañeda, A. 1974. *Cultural democracy, bicognitive development and education*. New York: Academic Press.

Sailor, W. 1972. Reinforcement and generalization of productive plural allomorphs in two retarded children. *Journal of Applied Behavior Analysis* 5: 183–90.

Sherman, J. 1971. Imitation and language development. In *Advances in child development*, eds. H. W. Reese and L. P. Lippset, pp. 239–72. New York: Academic Press.

Skinner, B. F. 1957. *Verbal behavior*. Englewood Cliffs, N.J.: Prentice-Hall.

Slobin, D. 1971. Developmental psycholinguistics. In *A survey of linguistic science*, ed. W. O. Dingwell, pp. 214–31. College Park, Md.: University of Maryland Linguistics Program.

Vygotsky, L. 1962. *Thought and language*. Cambridge, Mass.: MIT Press.

Weinreich, U. 1953. *Languages in contact*. New York: Linguistic Circle of New York.

Whitehurst, G. J. 1971. Generalized labeling on the basis of structural response classes. *Journal of Experimental Child Psychology* 12: 59–71.

Whitehurst, G. J. 1972. Production of novel and grammatical utterances by young children. *Journal of Experimental Child Psychology* 13: 502–15.

Index